Other books by the author
Walter F. Philbrick

Surviving

Twelve Rounds to Success

Dracula
Breed of Darkness

Ghost Witness

On Patrol

A police officer's experience in South Florida told through short stories

Lt. Walter Philbrick

authorHOUSE®

AuthorHouse™
1663 Liberty Drive
Bloomington, IN 47403
www.authorhouse.com
Phone: 833-262-8899

Published by AuthorHouse 10/26/2021

ISBN: 978-1-6655-1793-5 (sc)
ISBN: 978-1-6655-1792-8 (e)

Library of Congress Control Number: 2021903780

Print information available on the last page.

Any people depicted in stock imagery provided by Getty Images are models, and such images are being used for illustrative purposes only.
Certain stock imagery © Getty Images.

This book is printed on acid-free paper.

Contents

Acknowledgements

Being a police officer is not an easy job. It takes years of experience and on the job training to be a good cop. The impact your supervisors and training officers have on you as a rookie is extremely important to your development in becoming a good police officer. You will find it takes a good three to four years on the road before you really know what is happening out there on patrol. Every shift is a learning experience.

My first F.T.O. or Field Training Officer was Bill Connors. He taught me the difference between a criminal and a citizen. That is important at 2:00 am at night in an alley when you confront an individual. Are they friend or foe? Bill gave me insight into making a quick but rational decision on the suspect.

I want to thank Steve Hamel, my first sergeant, for taking the time to teach me how to be a productive police officer on duty. Thank you Steve.

After I made Sergeant I had several good Lieutenants and Captains. George Kartis and Larry Blankenship's influence taught me how to be a good supervisor and how to lead men. They set the standard of what ranking officers should do.

I should recognize my SWAT Team members. Lt. Ed Beyer had the confidence in me to handle any SWAT callout. He would look at me and say, "Philbrick, you got this." I will always appreciate the confidence you had in me to supervise the SWAT Team in lead the team on some really dangerous callouts.

Being a SWAT Team Leader was dangerous but fun. The dangers we encountered were daily and we stood as a team and survived. Every team member I served with should be proud for their service.

In closing, after more than 30 years in law enforcement, I want to thank my fellow police officer's for their friendship and dedication for being a "good cop."

For the rookie police officer reading this book, "Remember one thing, "At the end of your shift, make sure you always go home." And, one more piece of advice, "If you give respect, you will get respect." Treat the public as you would want to be treated.

About the Author: Walter Philbrick

I started my police career with the City of Hialeah in 1977. The city of Hialeah is a fairly large community just west of Miami Dade County and the City of Miami. I graduated from the South East Florida Institute of Criminal Justice which is also known as the police academy. At that time, that was the Police Academy for all law enforcement agencies in South Florida.

After graduating from the Police Academy all rookie police officers are assigned to a FTO or Field Training Officer for three months. After that you are assigned a shift and ride alone. I worked the midnight shift in Hialeah. After three years on patrol I was reassigned to a plain-clothes unit. The unit, called 1-A specialized in catching crimes in progress.

This undercover unit targeted crimes such as armed robberies, commercial and residential burglaries and auto thefts. It was a fun unit to be in because we apprehended hundreds of criminals. A majority of the time, we arrested the suspects while in the process of committing the crime.

The undercover unit proactively set up surveillances. We would study the daily crime reports and chart crime patterns. Then we would set up and wait for the criminals to arrive and many times that's just what happened. We would watch them committing a burglary or stealing a car and then tactically take them down.

In 1984, I was transferred to the detective bureau that investigated crimes against persons. In the detective bureau, I was promoted to the rank of Sergeant. As a homicide sergeant, I supervised a team of four or five homicide detectives that also investigated other crimes, specifically against persons. This included robbery, sexual battery, aggravated assaults, shootings, stabbings and other serious crimes.

During my 30 years in law enforcement, I was proud to be a member of the Hialeah Police SWAT Team for over thirteen years. I was assigned the duties of a SWAT Team leader and as the SWAT Team Training Coordinator. I was responsible for developing new and improved training for the SWAT Team. At that time, our SWAT Team consisted of twenty officers. As a supervisor and team leader, I can say that everyone on the SWAT Team was fearless. We were called out when the situation exceeded the capability of the patrol officers. Every call-out was high risk and extremely dangerous.

During my career, I also supervised a Vice and Narcotics unit, police training division, police honor guard and police communications. I was also a patrol officer and a sergeant in the uniform patrol division for several years.

During my tenure as a full-time police officer, I instructed at the Miami-Dade Police Academy for more than twelve years. I taught defensive tactics, use of force, officer survival, firearms and arrest techniques.

After twenty-two years of service, I retired from full-time duty as a police officer in 1999. I am still an active Reserve Police Lieutenant with the Hialeah Police Department. To keep my police certification active, I have to work a minimum of six shifts each year, qualify with my firearm and attend training classes.

I have appeared on the Today Show, 60 Minutes, CNN, ABC Primetime, the Learning Channel, Newsweek, Time Magazine and Good Housekeeping magazine as well as on numerous television shows and additional newspaper articles.

To order books signed by the author:

Walter Philbrick
1714 North Dixie Highway
Hollywood, Florida 33020
Phone: (954)-367-5591
Cell: (954)-895-4641
Email: Walter.Philbrick@Gmail.com

Introduction

The stories in this book are a culmination of 22 years of police work. All of the stories in this book are true. I did my best to research the cases and make them as accurate and truthful as possible. Although, it's been a long time and I may put an officer on scene when he really wasn't there. But the story itself is as factual as I can remember.

This book was written for those individuals who were police officers, or for anyone who is interested in law enforcement. You may want to be one of the select few individuals that wear the uniform, badge and gun when you go to work. It was an honor to serve the City of Hialeah for over thirty years as a Patrol Officer, Sergeant in Homicide, SWAT Team leader, Vice and Narcotics Supervisor, Police Trainer and now, as a reserve Police Lieutenant. Hopefully, after reading this book and the stories contained within it, you might find the job challenging and interesting enough to become a police officer. Then again, you might read it for educational and entertainment value. Either way, it's a pleasure to meet you through my stories.

Being a police officer has never been or will it ever be, an easy job. There are just too many variables. Whatever you do on and off duty is going to be scrutinized by your police administration, the courts, media and the video camera most officers are wearing on their vests today. Not only did the job get tougher, now there will be video recording of what you do on and off duty. Everyone has a camera. Welcome to the Millennium.

I started my police career in 1977. Most of you reading this book were not even born when I graduated the police academy. Everything has changed since then and hopefully, for the better. The law enforcement officer of today is better trained and equipped than I was forty years ago.

On my first tour of duty, my FTO or Field Training Officer was Bill Connors. The first thing he did was to show me where the call boxes were in our zone.

The police radios that we carried in the 70's worked sometimes, but not all the time. You actually had to bang them once in a while to get reception.

The Comco radios were so bad we had to rely on a telephone call box as a backup plan. The call box was a direct line to the police department. When you picked up the phone, it would ring in dispatch and someone in police communications would say, "Hialeah Police Department, how can I help you?" A lot has changed in the past forty years.

On my first night as a police officer, I was extremely excited. Prior to leaving the station, I checked out a Smith & Wesson 12-gauge shotgun. After roll call, Officer Connors and I were ready to get in our marked police unit and go on patrol. As we walked out of the station, Connors looked at me and said, "Rookie, you can drive" as he threw me the keys to the marked police car. I handed him the shotgun I had checked out. He loaded the shotgun with five rounds of buckshot.

I looked at the keys Officer Connors had given me. The brass key tag was numbered 6824. That was the number of our marked police unit. I quickly found out that the first two digits of the car key ring was the year of the vehicle. That's right, the car was nine years old.

After a few minutes searching the parking lot, I found the cart numbered 6824. The car was old and looked it. I got into the vehicle and immediately noticed the rusted floorboard had several holes in it and a rubber mat had been placed on the floor to keep out most of the exhaust fumes. The Hialeah police didn't have the best equipment back then. Connors locked the shotgun in a rack in front of the seat and said, "Let's roll!"

My first night of police work was slow. We conducted a few traffic stops and then the radio became silent. It was now around 2:30 am. After driving around, Officer Connors said to me, "I had court today and I'm tired. I'm going to catch a little shut eye for a few minutes. Listen, Philbrick, don't stop anybody or do anything stupid unless you wake me up first. Do you understand?" I said, "Yes sir, I do."

I liked the fact that he was sleeping. It was a lot like being on patrol alone. I didn't know what to do, so I just drove around waiting for dispatch to give us a call. I got through my first night without killing anybody and I had a good time.

That was a long time ago and everything about police work has changed. After reading this book, you may appreciate what a police officer does on a daily basis. It's the only job in America where there is a good chance you could get killed on your next shift. There are lots of stories in this book and every seasoned police officer has them, not just me.

There are some stories, statements and scenarios in this book you may find unprofessional, inappropriate and or humorous. Cops use profanity to escalate or diffuse a situation.

You will read exactly as it happened by myself or other officers on scene. It's just the way we communicated years ago. It's a different story today.

Hopefully, you will find the humor in the word spoken and remember it's a book written for entertainment, possibly educational and not proper ethics.

Every story or event written in this book is absolutely true. I have changed a few names of officers, witnesses, civilians, addresses and/or the general public for their protection. Some of the stories could quite possibly get the officer or witness in trouble, even after all these years. Also, some people did not want their names used in the story for personal reasons.

This book has been written based upon personal events, experiences in my life and extensive research including facts, laws, case law, criminal events, protective actions, and even defensive tactics that have saved my life. The contents of this book could possibly save your life. However, the reader should understand that each event will be different. I can't give you an exact checklist on how to survive. Therefore, the author assumes no liability or responsibility for the use or content of this book.

In a perfect world, there would be no crime or terrorist attacks. But we know differently. It is dangerous out there no matter what country you live in. I would like to be there if you are attacked or assaulted. But we both know that isn't going to happen. I obviously can't be there to help you, but this book can give you the tools to help you survive

I have provided several case studies, as well as personal experiences and circumstances that in some cases, saved my life as a police officer on the street, as a SWAT team leader and as a civilian. These experiences and case studies can give you some insight on what to do and how to react if you are threatened or attacked.

Everything changes by your actions and reactions. You have to react in a millisecond to survive. What you do at the time of attack will dictate whether you survive or not. Hopefully, after reading this book, you will understand what it takes to survive.

This book and any recommendations or case law are not rendered as legal opinion or advice. I am not an attorney and any opinion expressed by me is not a suggestive legal action or recommendation. Also, remember that laws are constantly changing.

I hope you enjoy my career and over 40 years of notable police work in this book.

Chapter One

Recruitment and Selection

Being a police officer has been described as 'Eight hours of boredom, interrupted by seconds of sheer terror.' As a police officer with over forty years of experience, I have been there. The new breed of law enforcement will face many changes, as well as new threats and crimes. Just to name one change is the body camera that records everything the officer does while on duty.

Events happen quickly when you are on duty or on patrol. From out of nowhere, you are attacked and have to defend yourself. If you don't use your experience, skills and training, you could be a statistic. That is why hiring the right person for the job is so important.

From the day you are hired to your first day in a patrol car, your police department has invested over $50,000 getting you trained and equipped. That is why the selection process is so important. Not everyone is cut out to be a police officer. You become a police officer, not for the pension or the health benefits. You become a police officer because you want to help and make a difference.

Being in law enforcement today is a challenge. In the past few months, there have been several random shootings of police officers sitting in restaurants or in patrol cars. The risk of being killed on duty is at an all-time high.

Working patrol is very different than being a homicide detective. It takes a special kind of person to be a police officer. Some of us have that quality and some don't. The police academy is just a stepping stone to your first day on the job.

A lot of people love watching police movies and the television crime dramas like CSI or Chicago P.D. In real life, that is not police work. We don't solve multiple homicides or get in three shootouts in one hour. That is made for TV drama which is highly entertaining and does give you some insight into law enforcement.

Very few people that apply for the position of police officer are selected. In my hiring class, over 600 took the civil service examination and more than half failed.

Of the 300 plus left over, more than half did not pass the psychological examination. Now, we are down to just over a hundred applicants. After the psychological exam, most police departments conduct a physical PT test where you have to run a mile and a quarter in under 12 minutes. After that, there is usually an agility test to include push-ups, sit-ups, rope climbing and an obstacle course.

Many of the applicants do not pass the physical test unless they have trained for it. More than half of the remaining applicants do not pass the physical test. Now, we are down to less than thirty or forty applicants from the original 600. At the end of all this, less than 5% are on the list to be hired.

The Police Department really does want to hire as many applicants as possible from the civil service exam group. It just doesn't happen.

The next step is the polygraph test or lie detector exam. This is where a lot of applicants fail, thinking they can beat the test. That doesn't happen. From the 40 remaining on average, the polygraph will weed out those who lied on their employment application. That is why, if you apply to be a law enforcement officer, you start telling the truth the day you fill out your application. One of the questions on the test is, "Have you been totally truthful on your application to be a police officer?" If you left out being fired from Publix for showing up late for work, it will come up during your polygraph test. Now you are down to about 20 or 25 from the 600.

Almost all pass the medical part of the process. In my class, we lost 2 due to color blindness and poor vision.

The last step, after all the tests, background checks, polygraphs and more is the oral interview. The police applicant will meet with a review panel of four high ranking police officers.

At the interview, you will be evaluated on your personal appearance, interview skills, presentation and your ability to answer some tough questions. Answer them truthfully. The answer is not as important as your ability to look calm and confident while under a little pressure.

After the interview, the candidates who pass are placed on an eligibility hiring list that rates them from 1 to 15. The department will select from that list, usually hiring 6 to 10 people.

The lucky 10 candidates survived all the tests and beat out more than 600 other applicants. If they knew their chances of being hired were about 1 out of 60, very few would have applied and gone through the process.

Congratulations! Now, all you have to do is pass the Police Academy.

Chapter Two

The Police Academy

The Police Academy usually takes about 18 weeks. That equates to 720 hours of basic law enforcement training. The academy's academics is based on a ninth- grade education. What does that tell you about how smart police officers are? But, once you are in the academy, the ninth-grade educational standard is not so easy to pass. Besides state laws, use of force, patrol procedures, defensive tactics, criminal law, driving skills and more, the academy is a tremendous learning tool for new police recruits.

The academics was good, but most academies lacked real world experience. That has changed in the last twenty years. Now, cadets actually ride with police officers while attending the academy.

Cadets are hired after taking a civil service test, a physical and psychological exam and more. The Police Academy is the secondary layer that weeds out candidates that should not be police officers.

Each academy class is assigned a TA or Training Advisor who is responsible for that particular BLE or Basic Law Enforcement Class. The TA is usually a sergeant or an officer with leadership skills. He or she has been on the road and looks and acts like a seasoned police officer. It is his or her responsibility to mold their BLE class into a working unit, while at the same time, evaluating each and every cadet's level of fitness for duty.

Most academy classes are 25 to 30 rookies, all trying to become certified police officers. Out of that class, on an average, 3 or 4 will not make it for various reasons. Some will fail academically, one or two are going to get injured and others have personal problems or other issues.

In the third week of my academy class, we were all sitting in the classroom and the instructor was showing us how to direct traffic at an intersection. About halfway through the lecture, two Miami Dade Police Officers walked into the room and whispered something into the instructor's ear. The instructor stopped the lecture and said, "Excuse me, BLE 36 but these officers are here to talk to trainee, Roberts. Officer Roberts, will you accompany these officers out into the hallway?" Trainee Roberts stands up and says, "I think I know what this is all about." He starts walking toward the front of the class and the instructor says, "Trainee Roberts, get your books, you will not be coming back."

Later, we found out that Trainee Roberts was wanted for Grand Theft Auto. When the instructor said, "Get your books, you won't be coming back," you could have heard a pin drop. That got everyone's attention in the class and we knew it was a privilege to be in the Police Academy.

On another occasion, one of the trainees arrived for defensive tactics not wearing his blue sweatshirt with his name and number on the back. He had a white t-shirt on. His name was Steve Avery. One of the instructors barked out a command, "Trainee Avery, where is your defensive tactics shirt?" When confronted by the instructor, he stated, "Sir, my dog chewed it up. I have to purchase another one." The instructor stated to the Trainee, "Change back into your uniform and I will meet you in a few minutes." Puzzled, the cadet went into the locker room to change.

After a few minutes, the Training Advisor and the instructor both walked into the gym together. Sergeant John Rock told the class, "Class, circle around." We are usually circled up on the mat to learn a new defensive tactic takedown. Not this time.

Sergeant Rock had the class wait until Trainee Avery rejoined his class in uniform. He nodded to the TA. TA Campbell walks from the back of the class to the front. He is carrying a black, plastic bag. He paused for a moment, took a deep breath and said, "As a police officer, or even a police recruit, our word or what we say must always be the truth. There must never be a compromise where telling a lie is better than being truthful. In your careers as police officers, you will be asked some tough questions and you must never waiver from telling the truth, no matter what the consequences are. Do we understand that?" The entire BLE class yelled, "Yes sir, we understand that."

Officer Campbell, holding the plastic bag, then stated, "Trainee Avery, please stand.

Trainee Avery says, "Yes sir."

Officer Campbell asks, "Trainee Avery, where is your BLE defensive tactics shirt with your name and class number on it?"

Avery, "Sir, my dog chewed it up. I could not wear it. I will get a new one today."

Campbell then says, "Your shirt has the name Avery on it, class BLE 36 and your trainee number, 18. Is that correct?"

Avery immediately responded, "Yes sir."

Campbell asked him again, "Number 18, where is your defensive tactics shirt?"

Avery responded loudly, "Sir, I have to replace it. My dog ate the shirt this morning and I couldn't wear it to class."

Campbell, "Are you telling God, country and your classmates the truth?"

Avery, "Yes sir."

Campbell, "Trainee Avery, you will not need to get a new defensive tactics shirt today. Do you know why?"

Avery, "No sir, I do not know why."

Campbell, "Avery, what is your class number?"

Avery, stood at attention, responded back, "Number 18, sir."

Officer Campbell then reached into the plastic bag and pulled out a blue, long sleeve, defensive tactics shirt. He held it up for the class to read the name on the back. On the back of the shirt was the name, AVERY with the student number 18.

You should have seen the look on Avery's face. He had left his shirt in the locker room last week and to cover up for not having his shirt, he fabricated the story that his dog chewed it up.

Campbell barks out the question, "Avery, is this your defensive tactics shirt?"

Avery responded, "Yes sir, I believe that is my shirt."

TA Campbell looked at Avery and said, "I am no longer going to address you by your trainee name or student number because you are no longer associated with this police academy. Mr. Avery, clean out your locker and report to my office.

He was terminated that day for lying to command staff.

The Police Academy roots out some of the bad guys who slipped through the hiring process but there were not that many. Ninety-eight percent of the police officers hired are honest and hard working. It's that two percent that gives cops a bad name. They seem to slip through the process and get hired and certified. But eventually they screw up and are recognized and eventfully terminated.

Once the cadet graduates the academy, most police departments have a one year probation period where the police trainee can be terminated. Many times the police trainee will be assigned to an FTO or Field Training Officer. Some times the officer will need extra training and cycle through the FTO Program more than one time. The department wants to retain the new cadet and will try several times in an attempt to keep the rookie police officer. Remember, the police department in most cases has invested close to a hundred thousand dollars hiring, training and certification of the new police officer. So the trainee may be assigned on the riding assignment a few times in an attempt to retain the rookie officer.

Chapter Three

"Hey Rookie"

Uniform Patrol Division

After graduating from the Police Academy, you are assigned to the uniform patrol division. Rookies go directly into a training program with an FTO or Field Training Officer. A seasoned veteran takes you under his or her wing and teaches you what the police academy didn't teach you about being a police officer. It is reality versus textbooks. The criminals have no rules, but we do. To survive on the street, you will quickly learn what keeps you alive as an officer on patrol. On your very first night as a police officer, you learn what really goes on in the streets of Miami or any other big city. This is something you can't learn in a textbook, classroom or in the academy. You are instructed that the most important rule in law enforcement is, that you go home at the end of your shift.

In the eighteen week police academy, the scenarios are controlled and scripted. The roll playing is designed to test the rookie police officer's ability to react to a specific threat or situation. That could be a traffic offender who just ran a red light, an irate husband and wife fighting, a bank robbery in progress or a suspicious person. Your job is to arrive, take control of the situation and resolve it.

As a rookie, you try to learn fast but in actuality, it takes a good 3 to 4 years of patrol experience to know exactly what is going on out there in your city or jurisdiction.

Some officers spend their entire career in patrol. This is not by choice, but because they may be disruptive, can't write a report or just don't want to be anywhere else. That makes sense sometimes. In patrol, you complete your shift and go home. There are no midnight phone calls asking you to explain what you did on a scene five hours ago. You put your time in and you are off duty till your next shift. It's an 8 to 5 job. When you are off, no one bothers you. I was in homicide for two and a half years. I was the sergeant of the unit and my phone rang every night at home. If there was a homicide or major crime case, I had to go back to work.

I have retired from full time active duty and currently work as a reserve police lieutenant. As a reserve officer, I have to ride a certain amount of days each year. In my department, reserves have to ride with another officer and not alone. That doesn't make much sense to me but that's the rule.

I will show up at roll call and the shift sergeant has to put me with somebody. Nobody wants me in their car. For that matter, other officers do not want a reserve officer, especially a lieutenant with them, period. The first reason they don't want me is now they have to move all their stuff from the front seat and secondly, I am going to mess up their night. They may have plans later in the night that they don't want me or anyone else to know about. That could be finding a hole and going to sleep, visit a girlfriend or boyfriend, doing some shopping between calls or other activities. The patrol officer has an agenda and really wants to ride alone. Sometimes the sector sergeant will say, "Philbrick, you're with me." That's ok with me.

It was rare for police officers to ride 'Two Man' in Hialeah. Why? Because, after midnight, one officer would be sleeping and the other would be driving. The one officer could have had court all day and be exhausted or he or she may have worked an off-duty job. Everyone understood that on midnights, it was better to find a buddy to crash with for a few minutes rather than be by yourself behind some warehouse. It was dangerous. I can tell you I drank a lot of Cuban coffee when I was tired. It was like jet fuel.

On one of my midnight shifts, my FTO said to me, "Listen, Philbrick, I had court all day and I'm tired. So you can drive but don't stop anyone. Don't get in any shit or take police action until you wake me up. Is that understood?" My reply was, "Yes sir." I was just excited to drive around the city almost by myself.

Roll Call

Roll Call was always entertaining. That is when you are assigned a patrol zone for that shift. I usually worked a ten-hour shift from 10pm to 8am. I would work 4 days and then have 3 days off. Every officer is given a zone to patrol with another officer. Sometimes, there will be three or four officers in a zone if it is big enough. You may be in separate cars, but were dispatched usually to the same call if it was in your zone.

Roll Call started promptly at 10:00 pm. Being late for roll call was inexcusable. You were expected to be on time, dressed in your uniform and ready to go 'in service' immediately after roll call ended.

Sometimes, during roll call, the sergeant or lieutenant would conduct roll call training. The topic could be use of force, new standard operating procedures or new federal guidelines on Miranda or other subjects.

Roll call would usually end with the shift lieutenant saying, "Let's go out there and have fun but be careful."

Chapter Four

Midnight Shift Patrol Division

Hunting

Being a police officer is dangerous, but it can also be a lot of fun. I would have gone to work my first ten years without pay. The challenge of catching the criminals and the camaraderie with the other officers made the job enjoyable and rewarding. This has changed a lot with the body cams and stricter guidelines on patrol procedures, but you can still do your job and have fun.

When the midnight shift officers arrive at the police station for 10pm roll call, most of the officers are excited to get started. We really enjoyed being police officers on midnights. This was the working shift. If someone stopped a car for being suspicious or a traffic infraction, another officer would always drive by to make sure that you were ok.

Why was it fun? First, all of the brass was gone. The police chief and most of the command staff were all home sleeping. The midnight shift consists primarily of a captain, one patrol lieutenant and three or four sergeants. On an average night, we would have 18 to 20 police officers also working the midnight shift. That would equate to about 4 or 5 men per zone. If a hot call was dispatched, half of the responding units were from the territorial zone next door to it.

Secondly, this group of men and women want to work. They can make a difference on this shift because, after midnight, there are only good guys and bad guys out there. Most of the good people are home sleeping. The criminals and bad guys welcome the darkness for cover while they work and commit crimes. Sometimes, I would just go to the warehouse area, turn my car off, get out and just listen. I have arrested several midnight burglars who thoughts they were alone.

When the midnight shift goes '09' or 'in service,' we go hunting. It is us against them. The good guys against the bad guys. My radar is up and I'm looking to put someone in jail. On midnights, crime is a little different. On this shift, the criminals commit crimes like auto theft, commercial burglaries and armed robberies. On the midnight shift, we don't hunt animals, we hunt men. Sometimes, dangerous men. The criminals are working also, and it is our job to outsmart them and put them in jail.

Here is a quote from a famous novelist that you will recognize. He said it best.

> **"There is no hunting like the hunting of man, and those who have hunted armed men long enough and like it, never care for anything else thereafter."**
>
> **Ernest Hemingway**

Anything that moves after 2am gets stopped, frisked and checked out. You have to remember that criminals work also. While you are home tucked away in bed, the rapists, robbers and thieves are just getting up to rob a convenient store or burglarize the cars in a parking lot of a condominium.

The problem with working midnights is you are tired most of the time. If you have court, you stayed up most of the day, testifying. After you get home, you try to get a few hours' sleep prior to your shift. Bottom line, you go to work tired. So what happens is you meet up with another officer in the warehouses and one of you will sleep for fifteen minutes while the other officer monitors the radio.

One night it was busy, so I wasn't tired until about three in the morning. I drank some Cuban coffee but that didn't work. I was exhausted. I called another officer in my zone and we met in a warehouse area. You always park facing opposite, so his driver's door is next to my driver's door.

It's easier to talk that way. My unit number was 2312 and the other officer's number was 2310. His name was Ted Zorksy. He said, "Wally, I'll cover the radio for twenty minutes and you get some sleep. I thanked Ted and I was out in minutes. It was 3:10 am. At 3:42, dispatch was sending out an emergency alert tone. It was a high-pitched tone that lets everyone know there is an emergency, a crime is in progress or an officer is down.

All I hear is the alert tone and my unit number. There is a long beep tone and then dispatch says, "2312, are you QRU? Which means are you ok? Then she raises the shift lieutenant and tells him, "Dispatch cannot raise 2312." I look at the time and its 3:43am. I jump up in my seat and look over at Zorksy. He is sound asleep. He had fallen asleep while covering for me. I raised dispatch and told them I was ok and just had radio problems. I woke Ted up and he just laughed. I was the one they couldn't find, not him.

Don't take the job home

I'm going to repeat this. The first rule of being a police officer is to make sure you go home after your shift. No matter how many fights, high speed chases or shootings you get involved in, at the end of your shift, you go home to your family.

For you future police officers, the second rule is, don't take the job home with you. What kept me on an even keel is that I kept my gun, uniform and badge in a locker at the station. I very rarely took it home. This was my way of leaving what happened at work, at work.

Raising a family and being a police officer is not easy. When I was in the academy, I remember the TA telling the new recruits, "If you have civilian friends, keep them." What he was telling us is that you don't want to have only police officers as your only friends. You need to relax with other people who are not in law enforcement.

As a police officer, and I say this with respect to all military veterans, it is difficult to just turn off the soldier or police officer within you when your shift ends. Man, some nights, you are fired up and just can't sleep. As a soldier or police officer, you are in harm's way every time you put on that uniform or strap that firearm to your side. To survive, you have to change your entire mentality in seconds, otherwise, you will not be prepared for duty. I tell myself after getting ready for duty, "It's time to rock!" That short little slogan changes my mental outlook and I am ready to go.

On this job, your friends get injured and killed. When I was single, with no children, of course I didn't want to get killed on duty, but if it happened, that is the luck of the draw. But, when you have people who depend on you and you are a daddy, putting your life in jeopardy or being killed is not an option. If you worry or think about this on the job, it's dangerous. As a police officer, you have to react to dangerous situations based on your instincts and not your emotions.

I was a member of the SWAT Team for over 13 years. First, as a team member and then as a team leader after my promotion to sergeant. With rank comes responsibility. Being a team leader put added pressure on me and our SWAT Commander. We had to get the job done. I had more experience in SWAT, so he would always say to me, "Philbrick, you got this?" Sometimes I wondered, was this more of a question than a command?

With fifteen SWAT team warriors, I felt we could handle anything. I had not fear and I would use my years of experience to get the job done without losing any team members. My priority was always team safety. We trained hard. As the SWAT team training coordinator, I changed a few things that the men didn't like. For example; on my first day, we trained in full gear. Nobody liked it. The heat, humidity, extra weight and full dress was heavy and cumbersome. You wouldn't go on a mission with just half of your gear so we trained ready for battle. The gear included your helmet, ballistic vest, sidearm, four 9mm magazines, stun grenade, AR-15 rifle, six 223 magazines, gas mask and carrier, first aid kit, knife, flashlight, radio and more. You weighed at least thirty more pounds. After a few months, the men quit bitching.

Patrol was dangerous but being on the SWAT team elevated that danger sometimes tenfold. Every call out had the potential of you getting shot or shooting someone else. During my time in SWAT, not a man on my team was killed. I can't say that for the bad guy.

On one operation, a psychotic, bi-polar individual who was also suicidal barricaded himself inside his apartment. Our negotiators tried to talk him out, but he was not coming out voluntarily. Therefore, we prepared to take him out. We were about to make entry, when all of a sudden, the thirty-year old male bolts out of the front door and slashes two team members with a knife before being shot and killed. If Officer Hart and Sergeant Beyer had not had on their bullet proof vests, they would have been seriously wounded. Even though he tried to kill two officers, I felt responsible for his death. We were there to save his life, not take it. But it was his decision. He controlled his own destiny. Hart and Beyer are exceptional SWAT team officers and they reacted as they were trained.

Chapter Five

Danger on the Job

Twenty Survival Tips

As a police officer, danger is part of the job. Every time you put on that uniform, there is a chance you won't be coming home that night. I should have been killed at least three times during my career. Experience and a little luck saved my life.

Just yesterday, I looked up police officers killed in the line of duty. Just last month, there were sixteen killed nationwide. That statistic would be higher if the police were not as well trained as they are and if they weren't wearing body armor. Kevlar has saved hundreds of police officers who may not have survived otherwise.

Just recently, in Las Vegas, two police officers were sitting in a restaurant, having lunch and were killed by a crazed gunman. He walked in and just started shooting.

What is the teaching point here? Even taking a lunch break can be dangerous. That is why you and I should always sit without backs to a wall. Even as a citizen, think like a police officer and always practice safety habits. If a threat arrives, you will be able to see it before it happens. Be alert at all times, even in a restaurant.

When I am at the station, getting dressed for work, the moment I put on that uniform, my mental attitude changes. I go from Wally Philbrick to Officer W. Philbrick. I immediately begin to be more aware of my surroundings and know that I am a walking target as soon as I put on my blues.

When I leave the house, I always give my son and wife a big hug. I know there is a small chance that I could be killed that day. With that in mind, I take the survival attitude and so should you. I never want my wife to get that phone call that I have been killed on duty. I made it a point to go home every night and I did for over thirty years.

Killed in the Line of Duty

During my tenure with the Hialeah Police, I took on the position of Honor Guard Sergeant. If an officer is killed in the line of duty or a retired officer dies and wishes to be buried with police honors, we will have a small but respectful police funeral.

The only problem I encountered was when a young officer died from cancer and his wife and girlfriend showed up at the funeral at the same time. He never told his girlfriend he was married. It was emotional fireworks for two or three minutes until I separated them. In the future, I did some background checking on the slain officer and his lifestyle, cleared out his locker and gathered up all his stuff from the police department. Once I went through it, I then gave it to the wife and his family.

As a police officer, I competed at the State Police Olympics, International Police Olympics and the World Games. All three events were very competitive and all of the competitors were police officers or fire fighters.

The State Police Olympics were every year and I usually competed in Judo, tennis and wrestling. It was a great place to meet other police officers, make friends and see them every year. It was a great excuse to get in shape and take a mini vacation.

The Police Olympics were hosted by different cities in Florida every year. If you won a medal, our department would reimburse you the lost time you took off to compete. Not a bad deal.

At the event, I would seek out old friends. The only problem was that some years, my police officer friends didn't show up because they had been killed in the line of duty. They wouldn't be competing that year of ever again. I took those deaths hard.

Police Officers get killed on duty due to a lot of circumstances. Sometimes it is just bad luck and other times, it's due to a critical or tactical mistake. If it's your fault, you will know that just before you are killed. You may be in a high-speed chase and get into an accident, killing yourself and an innocent bystander. Sometimes, it is better to let the offender go. Most chases end in horrific accidents and jeopardize the general public. But sometimes, you do everything right and still get killed.

A good example of that would be Peter Cainas. He was a Hialeah police officer who was killed in the line of duty. Peter Cainas was a good friend of mine on the job and also outside of work. We both were involved in Judo. Pete was a brown belt in Judo and practiced at my club at the YMCA in Hollywood many times. Officer Cainas was a police officer for several years and quit the department. He went to law school and became a lawyer. He practiced law for about eight years but missed the thrill and adventure of being a cop. Pete came back to work as a full-time police officer. He practiced law on the side.

One night, Officer Cainas and his partner responded to a domestic dispute on the second floor of an apartment building. There had been an argument with possible shots fired. On the night he was killed, he did everything right but still died. Here is what happened:

For precautionary safety, Pete knocked on the door and moved immediately away from the door and stood to the side. He was protected by a concrete wall. The subject, without provocation, fired his gun through the door at an oblique angle. The single shot struck Officer Cainas in the head. He could not have been in a better tactical position but the shooter shot almost parallel to the door. On this night, luck was not with him. He died two days later.

Emilio Miyares was another friend of mine who was killed on duty. There was a robbery in the mall and even though he was a motorman, he was the first officer to arrive. A Latin man with a Mac 10 machine gun robbed one of the businesses in the mall. Emilio ran into the mall and identified the armed robber. He fought with the subject but during the fight, the robber got hold of the officer's gun and ordered him to his knees. Witnesses said that Officer Miyares told the robber, "I have a family, please don't shoot." Seconds later, he executed the officer by shooting him in the head. The armed subject ran across the street into a housing development.

The SWAT team was called out to search a two-block residential neighborhood. It was a good size perimeter with about sixty houses in it.

The subject was armed and dangerous. I teamed up two SWAT officers with a K-9 unit. Patrol had a perimeter around the contained area. Due to the size of the area, Miami Dade Police sent out a helicopter for surveillance. I had a short meeting with the K-9 officers and the eight SWAT team members. I told them point blank, "If you get the opportunity, smoke this guy. He killed one of our own." Everyone agreed. I personally wasn't taking anyone in custody.

Forty-five minutes later, the armed subject was spotted by the police helicopter on the roof of a house on West 3rd Avenue. The SWAT Team quickly set up a perimeter around the house and evacuated nearby houses. I placed two snipers on the balcony of an apartment complex about one hundred yards away. We had him contained and trapped.

The helicopter reported the subject was laying down prone on top of the house. I got on the PA bull horn and told the subject to come down off the roof. At the same time four SWAT team members were quietly placing two ladders on one side of the roof. The subject could start shooting at the police helicopter or attempt to escape off the roof. He wasn't going anywhere.

I got on our PA bull horn and told the subject on the roof to come down or he would be extracted from the roof. We told him two times, once in English and then in Spanish. After a few minutes he stood up and surrendered.

He was taken into custody and charged with the murder of Emilio Miyares.

He plead guilty to killing Officer Miyares and was sentenced to 25 years to life.

Two F.B.I. Agents killed

On the early morning hours of Tuesday, February 2, 2021, five F.B.I. agents were shot while serving a search warrant for child pornography. Special Agents Laura Schwartzenberger and Dan Alfin were killed when the subject fired through the door killing both agents and wounding three other F.B.I. agents.

This is the second time in south Florida's notorious history that the Federal Bureau of Investigation lost two agents at the same time. On the morning of April 11, 1986, now called the FBI Miami Shootout, F.B.I. Agents Jerry Dove and Ben Grogan were killed and five more wounded when they attempted to arrest robbery subjects Michael Platt and William Matix.

The F.B.I. had been tracking Platt and Matix for weeks. At one time the Hialeah Police S.W.A.T. Team and the six F.B.I. agents were stationed near a bank that the two robbery subjects had surveilled the day before. We knew they were heavily armed and dangerous. The plan was to let them rob the bank and take them down as they exited. Unfortunately they failed to show and robbed a bank not in our jurisdiction.

Being a law enforcement officers has risks. In 2019 there were 135 police officers killed in the line of duty. But, in 2020, due to the COVID virus the number of deaths rose to a staggering number of 264 law enforcement officer's deaths due to work related injuries.

I survived more than 30 years of police work. These twenty survival tips can save your life.

Chapter Six

Detective Sergeant Homicide

I worked hard as a police officer in Patrol. I really enjoyed working midnights. In the early 80's there a tremendous amount of criminal activity when Cuba emptied their jail cells. Hundreds of Cuban immigrants arrived in South Florida from the Mariel Boat Lift. Almost all of them were released from Cuban jails. Most of these refugees were hardened criminals. Crime in South Florida skyrocketed to an all-time high.

Working patrol and being a police detective are entirely different. As a patrol officer I had the unique ability to seek out crimes in progress before anyone called the police. Sometimes, it was just plain luck and other times, just damn good police work. We have a saying in police work, "Even a blind squirrel gets lucky and finds an acorn once in a while."

With the thousands of Cuban refugees in the city of Hialeah, the murder rate jumped more than 400%. The drug wars were raging. The Cubans were killing the Puerto Ricans while the Columbian Cartel sat back and just watched. The price of cocaine doubled and so did the crime rate. It was Dodge City with gun fights every day. Our police department didn't have enough detectives to handle this unprecedented rise in crime.

As a patrol officer working your zone, sometimes you get lucky being at the right place at the right time. I was lucky more than one time. I probably fit into the detective bureau perfectly. I wrote a report on everything and anything. Some of the officers in patrol are lazy and don't do that. I was trained by my FTO (Field Training Officer), that if it was important enough for dispatch to send you there, then document it. That is what got me to the Detective Bureau. I was on the Sergeant's List and teaching at the academy. It was my fifth year as a police officer. I was at roll call and one of the lieutenants came up to me and said, "Congratulations, you're going to Homicide." I replied, "Lieutenant, I didn't put in for the detective bureau, there must be some mistake." The lieutenant replied, "From what I hear, you're going to DB." DB is the detective bureau.

Two weeks later, I was transferred to the Detective Bureau, Homicide Division. I was partnered up with Detective Eddie Royal who was one of the most experienced and best detectives in the police department.

I was promoted to sergeant two months later. My first year in homicide, we had 42 homicides. I think we solved 39 of them. Two still haunt me twenty-five years later.

I was a very busy Detective Sergeant. When someone is killed, the first forty-eight hours are critical. The TV program is a good example of being on the clock. People leave the city or state, evidence is lost, and your victim lives or dies. As a homicide sergeant, your team of investigators must produce or the case goes cold. And I mean cold fast. What happens is, there is another murder and you start working on that case and the first murder gets shuffled to the rear.

When I had a homicide in Hialeah, I would work until we produced something significant. I knew the 48-hour clock was ticking and every minute of every hour counted.

After a murder, before going home, I would meet with my homicide team of four or five detectives and debrief at around 2:00 am in the morning. I would go around the room and ask my team, "What do you have?" Many times, after going around the circle, I was told we have nothing. That didn't fare very well for me.

I would send them back out to find something. I would then reiterate to my team that we are not going home until someone produces a piece of significant evidence. I would say, "After ten hours of police work, you guys have nothing? Go out there and find something and don't come back until you have something of value."

Sometimes, I wouldn't go home for two days. I didn't care about the hours, I just wanted to find the shooter and many times, we did. The detectives I supervised were professional and wanted to solve the crime even more than I did.

Chapter Seven

Fear

I really didn't think about being killed or being afraid when I was a police officer until my son was born. Now the equation is just not me and my wife but an infant child. Having that responsibility made me more cautious when working.

What I enjoyed was the comradery with the SWAT Team members and other small groups of men and women. When you serve a high risk search warrant on a murder suspect knowing he may be armed and waiting for you, takes a special kind of person.

What makes it safe is knowing the guy in front of you or behind you has your back. If you go down, they will finish the job and get you out. You can't show any fear if you are a member of the SWAT Team.

I commend the men and women working today in law enforcement. Just yesterday an officer was killed in California. He was married and has three small children. That is why when I trained police officers, I made it tough. I wanted them to survive their shift and go home at night.

The Term Fear Reminds Me of a Story

One day, the martial arts Grand Master and his students were walking through the woods when the student noticed a fox chasing a rabbit. The student said, "Look, Master, the fox is chasing the rabbit." The Master asked the student, "What do you see, my son?" The student stopped and thought for a second and said to the Master, "The fox will surely catch the rabbit because he is much faster." The Master replied, "I'm not so sure, my son." The student replied, "Why is that, Master?" The Master answered, "Remember, my son, the fox is running for his dinner and the rabbit is running for his life. Who do you think will run faster?"

Author, Walter Philbrick: "I guess that is why I didn't catch many bad guys in foot chases."

The Police Officer and the Rabbit

I was dispatched to a residential burglary in progress. I arrived in the rear alley behind the building where the burglary was occurring. Just as I was parking and getting out of my marked police car, a female in her early 20s bolted out of the back door of the townhouse. The chase was on. The more I yelled, "Police Officer, stop! The faster she ran. I weighed 220 pounds plus I was carrying a Glock pistol on my right hip and an ankle holster with a .38 caliber revolver in it. With the extra weapons and gear on my person, I was carrying an additional ten pounds at least.

At the time, I was fairly fast for my age due to being in good shape from SWAT and Judo. However, the female was faster. I chased her over two fences and into an open field. After a few minutes, I was completely out of breath and had embarrassed myself on the police radio because I was unable to give the direction of the chase and the subject's description. I was so out of breath that dispatch could not understand a word I was saying.

As I chased the subject, I yelled, "Stop or I'll shoot!" I couldn't really shoot her, but I thought she might stop. She didn't. She just ran faster. I never gave up. I had been chasing her for five minutes now. After about a quarter of a mile, she started to slow down and I was getting closer. I yelled, "Stop or I'm going to beat your ass when I catch you." She didn't stop.

Dispatch is raising me on the radio, thinking I'm in trouble and a dozen police units flooded the area where I was before, not knowing where I was running to. I finally caught her when she fell over a kid's wagon in someone's front yard. I jumped on her. I was so tired, I couldn't even move. I had just enough strength to hold her down. I used my body weight to pin her on the ground until I could catch my breath and recover from the foot chase. She was saying, "Can you please get off me." I handcuffed her and stood her up. I didn't beat her ass. I wouldn't really do that, but it sounded good when she was running. I just wanted her to stop. I'm no track star.

Fear: Tactical Point

Here is the lesson: If you can run away from an attacker, then do it. Just keep running because he will get tired like the fox and stop chasing you. You are not an easy target if you are moving or resisting. If you are fighting for your life, don't give up. I chased a subject because it was my job. I never gave up on the foot chase. But if you are being assaulted or attacked, keep fighting until you can't fight anymore. Just when you want to quit, is the time things might just get better for you.

Chapter Eight

Short Police Stories

8.1   The Gun in the Newspaper

It was late at night and I was working commercial burglaries in zone one, one of our industrial areas. I was in the industrial district and as usual, dressed in plain clothes. This night, I was patrolling the warehouses close to the railroad tracks in Hialeah in an unmarked vehicle. It was about 3:00 am and I had just been through this commercial warehouse area not more than an hour before. This time, I noticed something different at the rear of the Suave Shoe warehouse. There was a green Volkswagen Beetle parked near the rear exit fenced gate. It appeared to be unoccupied. It wasn't parked there forty minutes ago.

I pulled up and parked my unmarked police unit just behind the suspicious vehicle. I focused my car's high beams on the Volkswagen. I was just about to get out when a little voice told me, "Walter, take this one with extreme caution."

In my years as a police officer, I have approached hundreds, if not thousands of suspicious vehicles. But for some reason, my survival instincts kicked in and I listened to that little voice in my head. "Walter, be extremely careful, this one feels different." You are not sure why, but you know that sixth sense has peaked and alerted you to an unknown danger.

I exited my vehicle and immediately went to the rear of my car and around to the passenger side door. My bright lights were still illuminating the Volkswagen and I could see inside of the vehicle. It was not occupied. That meant the subject and/or driver was out on foot and probably watching me.

Instinctively, I got down behind my vehicle near the passenger door. I unsnapped my holster and drew my Glock 9mm, semi-automatic pistol out its holster. I couldn't see him, but I felt that he was very near. That's when I yelled, "Police officer, come here. I see you over there in the bushes." Immediately after saying that, I observed a human figure jump up and start running southbound along a chain link fence. For some reason, I didn't chase him. I immediately called for backup.

That little voice kept me from danger. The subject was waiting for me to approach the suspicious vehicle. If I had, I would have had my back to him. He could have shot me from behind and I would never have seen him.

Responding officers set a perimeter around the area, but they could not locate the suspect. He fled on foot through the rear of the warehouse. First of all, I didn't have a description of the subject. All I knew was that he was wearing dark clothing. I looked inside the Volkswagen and in the back seat you could see bolt cutters, sledgehammers, lock pulls and gloves…tools and gear for committing burglaries.

At this point, all I had was a suspicious vehicle and an unknown suspect that fled, which is essentially nothing. After an hour of searching the area for the subject, all units went back to their assigned zones. I had the car towed, wrote a suspicious vehicle report and cleared from the scene.

I drove west to Lejeune Road. When I stopped at a red light at East 8th Avenue, I observed a man sitting on a bus bench. It was 4:12 am. Buses usually don't start running till around 7 or 8 in the morning.

I parked and requested another officer from my unit to back me up. A few minutes later, Sandy Flutie arrived. I told him about the Volkswagen and someone running. We were both in the same plain clothes unit.

We walked over to the Latin male on the bus bench to ask him why he was there at 4 o'clock in the morning. I could see his clothes were soaked from sweat. He was wearing a dark blue long sleeved shirt and work pants. The guy looked like he had just run a marathon. Even though it was cold and in the middle of the nights, he was sweating. He had no ID and told me his name was Rudy Mendez. I asked him why he was sweating and he stated he had left a bar and was going to jog home, but he got tired so he called a friend to pick him up. About that time, a green Ford Mustang pulled up. Rudy knew the driver. I really did not have any probable cause to detain him, so I let him go. He got in the car and they drove away.

After they drove away, I looked at the bus bench and noticed that the guy had forgotten his newspaper. I walked over, lifted up the newspaper and wrapped inside the paper was a loaded .45 caliber Colt semi-automatic pistol. He had been sitting there with the gun and hid it as I pulled up in my police car.

Quickly, Officer Flutie and I agreed that maybe he would come back for the gun. We drove across the street, hid our vehicles and concealed ourselves in the bushes. We could still see the newspaper on the bench. We were sixty feet away from the bus bench and the pistol.

After about five minutes, the green Mustang returned and parked on the corner. The driver stayed in the car while Rodolfo exited the Mustang and ran over to the bus bench. He reached under the newspaper and picked up the pistol. He then jammed it in his waistband and turned to run back to the waiting vehicle.

At this time, Sandy and I both have our guns drawn and are approaching the armed subject. We are both commanding the subject to go to the ground and not touch the pistol in his waistband. I'm yelling at the top of my lungs, "Put your hands up and get on the ground!" The subject thinks we are going to kill him and he drops to the ground. I handcuffed him and immediately reached into his waistband and removed the loaded firearm from him. At this same time, two other officers are taking down the driver of the Mustang.

After handcuffing the subject with the gun, I searched him. Guess what I found in his pocket? The keys to the Volkswagen parked behind the warehouse. He was the subject that ran after I pretended to see him in the bushes.

Sandy and I booked Rodolfo Mendez. We impounded the .45 pistol and cross referenced the towed Volkswagen to his arrest. We both knew that Mendez wasn't his real name but we knew that Miami Dad Police would not release him until they took fingerprints and ran him through NCIC and got a true identity.

I went home around 9:00 am that morning after I completed all of the arrest reports for the subject with the gun. He went to Dade County jail and I went home to sleep. The phone rang around 10:30 am, waking me up. Miami Dade Police are on the phone. The sergeant asked me who I arrested last night for carrying the concealed firearm and possession of burglary tools. I told him, Rodolfo Mendez. He corrected me with a different name. The subject had no ID when I arrested him. At the jail, every prisoner with no ID stays until the police can verify who they are. Miami Dade took his fingerprints and ran him in the NCIC computer. The sergeant asked me, "Did you arrest him?" I replied, "Yes sir, is he somebody important?" The sergeant then says, "You are a lucky man to have arrested him and still be alive." Puzzled, I asked, "Sarge, why is that?" He replied, "We ran him and got a hit. He is currently wanted for seven homicides in South Florida and maybe more. We have positively identified him as a suspect in five home invasion robberies and is also wanted in Puerto Rico for killing another drug dealer and taking his narcotics and cash."

Do you think he would have hesitated to kill me if I had approached his parked Volkswagen? He would have killed me. I got lucky this time. That little voice in my head saved my life that cold December morning.

The Gun in the Newspaper: Survival Point

So, readers, listen to your instincts. My instincts again prevented him from killing me. It doesn't matter where or when you get that 'feeling.' But when you do, please don't disregard it. Listen to that little voice in your subconscious. React; it could save your life.

After the arrest, Sandy and I talked about what we didn't do. What is that? Think about it for just one minute. What we didn't do was unload the gun from the newspaper when we left it on the bus bench. We let this killer pick up a loaded .45 automatic pistol. I will not make that mistake again. Hey, even cops are not always perfect but we learn from our mistakes.

8.2   Fire and Ejection

One night I was riding with Officer Larry Freeman. We were in an unmarked vehicle and he was driving. A new Cadillac passed us as we were driving southbound on Palm Avenue. We both looked at the driver and passenger at the same time. We looked at each other and said at the same time, "stolen car." It was obvious that the occupants were not the owners of the brand new Cadillac. They looked like crack addicts.

I said to Larry, "Let's stop them." He replied, "Let's run the tag first." I got on the radio, "705." Dispatch came back with "QSK." I was a sergeant and my unit number was '705' and QSK is the police code for 'go ahead.' I ran the tag on the Cadillac and immediately, dispatch raised me and said, "Is the vehicle occupied? It's a 22. A 22 is code for a stolen vehicle. I told dispatch the car was occupied by two males. The Cadillac was stolen.

Larry said, "OK, let's do it." I put the blue light on the dash and plugged it in the cigarette lighter. Immediately, the driver looked back and accelerated. The passenger leaned out the window and looked at us as we gave chase.

Larry accelerated as we passed 21st Street. The Cadillac was about 30 yards in front of us as we were in pursuit. Both vehicles were now going about 80 miles an hour. Thank God it was 12:20 am and Palm Avenue traffic was at a minimum.

The chase didn't last very long. The driver attempted to make a right turn and lost control of the vehicle. The white Cadillac veered off the road, hitting a fire hydrant and then a mound of dirt. When the vehicle ran over the fire hydrant, water started spurting out of the broken water line about thirty feet in the air. At the same time, the stolen vehicle's gas tank was torn out from underneath the carriage of the Cadillac and roared across Palm Avenue as it ignited, sending flames six to ten feet in the air.

So, let me set this up for you….The vehicle was airborne after hitting the fire hydrant and the dirt mound. There was a thirty foot cascade of water pouring out of the broken fire hydrant and at the same time, the gas tank was torn out from underneath the car and was sliding across Palm Avenue on fire. It was like a movie set. It couldn't have been choreographed better. But that's not all. The stolen Cadillac was now airborne about eight feet in the air as it came down hitting a brick wall. The passenger who was not wearing a seat belt was ejected out the side window as the car hit the wall and jackknifed sideways. The driver was still behind the wheel. When the car came to a stop, the passenger was thrown about twenty-five feet in the air and landed in the middle of the street. He died on impact.

As I exited the vehicle, I yelled to Larry, "Larry, check out the guy in the road; I'll take the driver." I pulled my Glock 8mm out and maneuvered around the gasoline burning in the road and approached the Cadillac.

As I approached the driver's door, I yelled, "Police Officer, put your hands up where I can see them." The driver was bloodied, but conscious. I opened the driver's door, reached over and unlocked his seat belt and dragged him out of the vehicle and onto the pavement. I rolled him over on his stomach and handcuffed him as he began screaming. I could hear Larry behind me. He was checking the subject that was thrown out of the vehicle. I heard, "Sarge, this one is dead." I was on the radio asking for fire rescue and a traffic unit to handle this traffic accident and fatality. The driver was still screaming as he laid face down, handcuffed. I looked at him and just shook my head. Now, I have a shit-load of paperwork to do. We had a stolen vehicle, a traffic accident, a fatality, property damage to the wall and hotel shrubbery, and a broken water main. Not to mention the driver who was still screaming. He only spoke Spanish but I could tell that he was calling me a whore, faggot and some other kind words.

Fire Rescue arrived. Later, at the hospital, I was told he had two broken arms, fractured ribs and a broken pelvic bone. I guess that was why he was upset at me for handcuffing him. He was charged with auto theft and vehicular homicide due to his friend dying. He pled to four years and was back on the street after serving just over two and a half years in prison.

Fire and Ejection: Tactical Point

I didn't think our little adventure would turn out to be an accident straight out of the movies in Hollywood. In police work, or as a civilian, expect the unexpected.

8.3   Hey, "Taxi"

It was just after midnight and I was southbound on Le June Road. I was in a marked police unit that was marked 'Sergeant' on the side, letting the public know that I was a supervisor. A slight rain was beginning. As I was approaching 41st. Street, an elderly female stepped into the road and flagged me down. I pulled over.

She opened the right passenger rear door and got in. It was beginning to rain so I thought nothing of it. I reached up with my right hand and moved the sliding plexi-glass divider so I could hear her. She said, "Can you take me to 826 East 14th. Street?" I replied, "Are you in distress or need anything medically related?" She looked at me and said, "Can you just take me to that address, please?" I wasn't too busy so I replied, "My pleasure. It will be just a few minutes."

Whenever you transport a female, you have to advise dispatch where you are starting from, your mileage and the address of where you are going. I raised dispatch, "2301, I will be transporting a female from East 8th Street to East 14th. Street. Mileage, 23,481."

It only took a minute to get her there and upon arrival, I got out and opened the rear door so she could get out. The rear doors cannot be opened from inside the vehicle so prisoners cannot escape. I closed the door and she was just standing there. She then reached into her purse and said to me, "How much do I owe you?" A little stunned, I said to her, "It was my pleasure and have a safe night." Again, she reached into her purse and came out with three dollars and handed it to me and said, "Well, the least I can do is tip you."

That's when it hit me. I said, "Who do you think I am?" She replied, 'You're a taxi cab company, aren't you? You can't work for free." She thought she flagged down a taxi, not a police officer.

I then said, "Miss, I'm a police officer." She backed up and looked at the side of my police car that read, 'Hialeah Police.' She then said, "Oh, my God, I am so sorry. I thought I was flagging down a cab."

She apologized and I had a good story to tell. I gave her back her three dollars.

8.4   In Service White Team

The Miami racial riots began on the evening of May 17, 1880. Four white Miami Dade Police officers were acquitted in the shooting death of a black male named Arthur McDuffie.

The riots started in Over Town, a subdivision of Miami. Soon thereafter, the looting and shooting was moving west to Hialeah. We did everything possible to contain the looting, shootings and fires. The Police Chief set a perimeter on the east side of the city. Police officers were stationed on NW 37th Avenue and controlled vehicular access to Miami and Hialeah.

A select few African American citizens in areas of Miami were shooting white people. Several tourists got lost and were killed. The residents in the area of Northwest 27 Avenue and 79 Street were shooting into cars, burning down businesses and attacking any police vehicle that came to the aid of anyone in danger. It was a war zone.

Every police officer on the Hialeah Police Department was ordered to report for duty. All police personnel would be working 12 hour shifts. The 12 hours shifts were called Alpha and Bravo. Everyone works 12 hours and then off for 12 hours and then back on until the civil unrest is over.

The Police Chief came to roll call and addressed the midnight shift patrol division. He stood in front of 35 to 40 police officers and said, "Men and women, it's going crazy out there. Certain areas of Miami are engulfed in flames as the riots continue. Innocent people are being killed because of the color of their skin. We are going to protect the citizens of Hialeah and let them burn their city down if that's what they want to do. Prior to going 09, (number code for going in service), I want you to go home and bring whatever firearms you have at home back to work. You are going to need them. That's it, be careful out there."

As the officers were going 'in service', they would raise dispatch and give their unit number and the code, 09. It sounded like this, "2312...09." Dispatch would repeat the sequence, letting the officer know he was now available for calls. Well, for the most part, they would be available for calls, but not everyone.

Officer Tom Nevins raised dispatch as he drove out of the police station. He said, "2322." Dispatch then raised him back, and Nevins said, "2322, 09 white team."

The air was quiet for a minute until you heard the patrol captain order Officer Nevins back to the station. He was disciplined for his racial remark.

In Service White Team: Teaching Point

Not professional. As a police officer, you represent your police department, the people in the city you work for and yourself as a professional police officer. There is no room for racial comments regardless of the situation.

8.5   Nut Cracker

I was riding with my second FTO, Tommy Johnson, on the midnight shift when we stopped a suspicious vehicle. There were two white males and one black male in the car. We got all three males out of the vehicle.

In the early eighties, when you saw a 'salt and pepper' team, it was always going to be a problem. We patted them down for weapons and started to interview them. One of them looked familiar to me and after a few minutes, the rookie, that's me, recognizes him and says to the white male, "Aren't you Dave Henderson with the...." That's as far as I got because the FTO hit me in the nuts with his flashlight. I had just identified an undercover officer to two subjects he was trying to purchase drugs from. I didn't get a chance to finish the sentence "with the narcotics division?"

I was in too much pain as I walked away and got into the patrol car. Later, I learned that you never say hello or talk to an undercover officer unless he or she acknowledges you first. I think my left testicle still hurts.

As a rookie, you ride with a Field Training Officer for three months. The three shifts are days, afternoons and midnights. After the eighteen weeks in the academy and three months on the road with an FTO, you finally get to ride by yourself on patrol. It is an exhilarating feeling when you get into your marked patrol car and leave the station alone. It's you and the bad guys.

Nut Cracker: Teaching Point

Many time, working undercover in plain clothes, I will be out of the city of Hialeah and may recognize other agency police officers working undercover. I have to remember that unless I am deputized, I am only a police officer in the jurisdiction I work in. From that day forward, if I ever saw a police officer that I recognized and not in uniform, I would never acknowledge them. UC or undercover protocol is, they have to acknowledge you first. Then you can converse with the UC operative or undercover police officer.

8.6   Car Thief with a Grocery List

One day, I was conducting surveillance with my SWAT-Tac team at the Westland Mall in Hialeah, Florida. I was working plain clothes in an unmarked vehicle.

There had been several armed robberies in the mall recently during a ten day period. The surveillance team had positioned themselves in the mall so we could cover most of the exits. I was assigned to watch the south entrance of the Burdines department store.

After sitting there for twenty minutes, I observed a tow truck circling the area for about five minutes. The male driver was driving up and down several rows of parked cars. Finally, he stopped the wrecker and backed up to a brand new dark blue Chevrolet Corvette with Colorado tags.

The driver got out and started putting chains on the vehicle to tow it. This was very suspicious behavior because the owner was not at the scene and the car had an out of state license plate. I called for a marked police unit to back me up. I then walked over to ask him, "What he was doing?"

When I got there, the driver was under the Corvette, putting the chains in place to tow the vehicle. I identified myself as a police officer and asked him to come out from under the car. You don't get any respect when you are in plain clothes with just a badge around your neck. At that moment, the uniformed patrol unit arrived.

When he got up, I asked him a few simple questions and he couldn't give me a straight answer to any of them. One question was, "Why are you towing this car from Colorado?" It was plainly obvious that he was attempting to steal the Corvette. When he couldn't show me a manifest or tow sheet for the Corvette, I arrested him for grand theft auto. When you make an arrest, you have to impound their vehicle also. After I searched and impounded his truck, I found a check list for twenty vehicles on the front seat.

The thief had been given a 'wish list' of cars that were needed by the chop shops he worked for. Chop shops are vehicle accident repair shops that steal cars for auto parts. Each car was described in detail with a description of the year, model, and the color of vehicle that someone had ordered. This was, in essence, a grocery list of cars that the thief needed to steal. One of the vehicles needed was a Chevrolet Corvette.

I always have had a good rapport with anyone I arrested. Why, because

I always treated everyone with respect and that included murderers, rapists and thieves. The thief I arrested was a professional auto thief. Every day, his job was to steal cars that were needed for body work or cars that had been in accidents. He would steal the exact make, model, color and year of the car damaged in an accident and the chop shop would replace the damaged parts. Who would know after the repair that the car parts were used and not new?

Every day, he would get in his tow truck and steal cars. He later told me that he was paid $400 for each car he stole on the list. He only worked three days a week and made more than $3,000 in cash every week. To him, this was a reasonable job and a good way to make a living.

Car Thief: Tactical Point

Lock your vehicle and leave nothing on your seats that is valuable. If it looks inviting from the outside, burglars will break into your car. I never park my car at the movies, shopping mall or a store unless I can see my car from the entrance to the mall or movie theater

8.7   A Drunk in a Bar with a Knife

One night working patrol, I was dispatched to a fight at one of our local red neck bars. This was one of our cowboy watering holes and there were fights in the bar all the time. Just prior to arriving, dispatch advised that one of the subjects was armed with a knife. A victim had been cut and fire rescue was on route.

I arrived on scene first and entered the bar alone. My backup was about a half mile away. If the subject was still cutting people, he had to be stopped. I did not draw my service weapon due to the fact that the bar was extremely crowded. In this country wester bar, there must have been more than 300 people in this small building.

As I moved through the crowd, people kept pointing at one of the patrons who was standing at the bar. He was facing away from me, holding a drink in his right hand. Prior to my arrival, I was told he had fought with another man and was losing the fight. He then pulled a knife from his back pocket and stabbed the other person in their right arm.

I identified the person everyone was pointing to. In a commanding voice, I said, "Police officer, do not turn around. Put both hands on the bar in front of you." I didn't want him facing me if he still had the knife. When I said that, he turned and immediately took a boxer's fighting position. He then threw his shot glass on the floor and growled, "I didn't do anything." I looked at both of his hands and they were both closed in a tight fist. He had put the knife back in his pocket.

I had just enough time to react when he charged me. He was pretty drunk and threw a right hook punch at me. Because I am a martial artist, I just moved away from his aggression and stepped back. That is called 'Open the door technique.' He lost balance and turned to attack me again.

At this point, I'm on him. Using a pressure point, I stopped his second attack and forced him to the ground. I maintained the pressure point until I had him handcuffed.

I transported him to the jail at Miami Dade County. They ran his prints and background. He was wanted for several armed robberies throughout South Florida.

Drunk in the Bar with a Knife: Tactical Point

The point of the story is, when he threw that shot glass on the floor and took a boxer's position, I knew the fight was on. The good thing for me was that he was extremely intoxicated and I was able to control him due to my years of martial arts training. I used the pre-attack clues and looked for aggressive movements just prior to him attacking me. In this case, I recognized the body language and it saved me from being in a fight and possibly getting injured. When you feel as though you are in danger and can see the attacker, watch the person's hands. Can you see both of his hands? Does he or she have a weapon? Look at body positioning and listen to the words being spoken. What is he or she doing and saying? You don't have much time. Very quickly assess the situation and ask yourself, "What is his body saying to me and what is he about to do?" That is why it is important to keep that reactionary zone or safe space between you and the attacker. That safe space is the 4 to 6 feet between you and the attacker. This will give you time to react when they attack.

8.8   Breathe for Control

As a sergeant on the SWAT team, I was usually the team leader. When I arrived on a scene, I had to be in control and immediately assume my position as the team leader or officer in charge. When I stepped out of my police vehicle, I had to look as though I was in command, immediately take charge and start telling team members their assignments for this mission.

Many times, driving to the scene where the SWAT team was staged, I had difficulty controlling my breathing. I was excited, but at the same time, a little nervous and I had some fear. A SWAT callout is usually for something serious like an officer being shot, barricaded subjects, or other emergencies where the patrol officers couldn't handle the situation.

While I was driving to the scene from home, the police dispatchers would update me on what was happening. One night, a police officer was shot at from a moving van. The three subjects had automatic weapons, and when the officer tried to stop them after a robbery, they shot at the patrol officer.

SWAT was being called out to search an area for the armed subjects. I got pretty excited driving there. My adrenaline was really pumping and I had a thousand things to do upon arrival.

I pulled up to the scene, stopped the car, and took five deep breaths. This took about ten seconds. I then exited my vehicle and took command of the scene. I had complete control of my breathing and most importantly, myself. How can I lead armed men if I can't control myself?

On this particular night, we did arrest the robbery subjects who shot at the officer. We called in the K-8 dog units and searched a six block area, arresting two of the three armed subjects.

During the area search, one of the dogs alerted on an area covered with dense foliage. We quickly surrounded the small wooded area and pointed our guns where the dog was telling us a subject was hiding. When we were all in position, I told the subject, "We know where you are. Drop your weapon and come out with your hands up. If you don't come out, I am letting the K-8 dog loose." It was perfect. Just after I said that, the dog started barking. Two other SWAT officers and I were pointing our weapons at this busy area. I could see a large pile of leaves. He was probably in there. The dog was alerting and barking. Suddenly, from behind us, about fifteen feet, I heard a voice say, "Don't shoot, I'm coming out."

We all turned around and this guy was getting up from the ground with his hands in the air. He had been hiding underneath a large pile of leaves and bushes behind us. He thought we had been yelling at him. We weren't. The K-8 dog had failed to locate him under the leaves and alerted on another area where nobody was. We quickly pointed our guns in his direction and placed him in handcuffs.

The worst part of the night was that he was laying on a fully loaded Mac-10 machine gun. If he had wanted to, he could have killed all of us. After that, I never completely trusted K-8 searches again. Dogs are not perfect.

Physical Reactions

It's good to be afraid. Fear promotes certain physical and biological reactions in the body. The body will respond to fear when you are scared. Have you ever felt that weak feeling in your knees? Your body begins to tremble and shake just a little. Your heartbeat increases and suddenly you have trouble breathing. To react to a threat now would be extremely difficult. Fear has gripped your body and you are frozen and can't move.

Some animals detect danger before it arrives. Their senses become heightened to a potential threat. We can also strengthen our warning system through practice and training. There have been clinical studies of the human brain that demonstrate that the cortex in the front of the brain can detect changes in the environment, which could affect our chances for survival. When your senses are heightened, your sense of smell and vision also intensify.

To train yourself to react under fear, you must experience the same conditions and feelings, time and time again. This can be done through real life experiences or training. Only through constant repetitions can you work your way through the fear and control your physical reactions.

8.9   No Fear

Why is the feeling of fear good? Because it increases your senses and kick starts your adrenaline. It also prepares your body for battle. You will think faster, react more quickly and make better decisions. During my tenure in SWAT, I was one of the team leaders for over ten years. Due to my experience, I handled most callouts.

On every SWAT operation, I had some fear, not gripping fear, but enough to know that I was going into battle and I had to be at my best. Our SWAT operations included barricaded subjects, arrests of serial killers and wanted murderers, hostage situations, serving narcotic, 'no knock' search warrants, entering into an apartment occupied by an armed police officer who killed nine people, high-risk vehicle take-downs, suicides, armed robberies and burglaries in progress and more.

One day, an hour before a SWAT mission, I was suiting up (getting dressed for the SWAT callout), and I realized that I was no longer afraid. We were going to arrest a homicide subject wanted in the city of Miami. I had lost the fear factor. I was no longer afraid that today I might get shot or even killed. I just wanted to complete the mission, debrief, and then go eat somewhere with the team. Was I becoming a danger to the team? That was when I knew it was time to leave the SWAT team. I was no longer scared prior to an operation. My adrenaline pump was just not pumping anymore. It was just another routine SWAT operation. There is never anything routine about police work, especially conducting dangerous SWAT operations. I left the SWAT team three months later after I was

I retired from the police department five months after my decision to leave SWAT. My career as a full-time law enforcement officer had ended. I was 47 years old. It was time to do something different in my life.

No Fear: Tactical Point

Adrenaline is a good thing. It will juice your body above normal conditions. Learn to use it for your advantage.

1932 FDR's First Inaugural Address. Franklin D. Roosevelt said,

"The only thing we have to fear is fear itself."

Or lack of fear, in my case.

8.10 Be Like Water

Bruce Lee, the martial artist and movie icon instructed his karate students to be like water. He was the master of his own style called Jeet Kune Do. Bruce Lee incorporated all the martial art styles into his system. What exactly does 'be like water' mean?

Water, by itself is one of the most powerful and destructive forces on the earth. After many years, running water can carve out mountains, create valleys and give deserts life. Water is pure and simple but an effective force.

When Bruce Lee said, "Be Like Water," he meant, "When you are fighting, your defense and attacks should be flexible and formless." As a martial arts instructor, he talked about the effortless running of water and how it matches and changes its shape to get through the smallest cracks. He taught his students not to study just one form of karate but to study all styles and perfect the style that fits you best.

You can change your style and techniques to defeat any attacker. Bruce Lee said, "My movement is a result of your movement. Water can flow or it can crash." If and when you are attacked, respond to the movements of the attacker. Your defenses must be reactive to the attacker and at the same time, anticipating their move. Like water, don't meet the force head on, go around and deflect the attack. Always remember, you have all the time to defend yourself, where the attacker is always in a hurry. They want to end the attack or robbery as soon as possible before someone calls the police.

But remember this… One of the most important factors, when and if you decide to fight, is your location. Is the road well-travelled, can someone hear you scream or are you alone on a desolate highway?

As police officers, we must win every time we are challenged, attacked or tested by the criminal element. If I am killed or injured, the attacker can get my firearm and kill other responding police officers. Therefore, it is my responsibility to be able to defend myself.

Be Like Water: Learning Point

This also applies to you as a parent. You must protect your children and your family. The circle of protection is not just from criminals but from anything that can injure, harm or endanger your family. This could be a hurricane, tornado or a home invasion robbery.

For now, let's concentrate on staying alive if you are attacked by an armed robber or a criminal. Dying is not an option. Your overall objective is to survive the attack, doing whatever it takes to live.

We have discussed that planning and preparing are two necessary steps to defend yourself and your family. It begins weeks, months, and even years before the actual attack. It is a slow and methodical progression to have the ability to know what to do and when to do it. Every attack is different and your response will most likely be dictated by the criminal.

You have to ask yourself, "What is the criminal's intent here? What does he want and what is he going to do?" If the robber just wants your money, give it to him! If he wants your new Rolex watch and your wife's purse, give it to him! During the robbery or attack, if you perceive that he is going to kill you or separate you from your wife or children, then you have a problem. It's time to take a stand. An action, not a reaction, on your part may decide whether you live or die. Be like water.

8.11 Close Shave

In Hialeah, near Red Road, sits a string of rental apartments. On this day, Rolando, a Latin male in his mid-twenties pulled into the apartment complex. It was around 2:30 pm. He was there to visit his new girlfriend who he has been seeing for about 2 weeks.

Unknown to him, the girl's ex was back in town. The boyfriend confronted her and she told him everything. The jealous ex-boyfriend, Alberto Mena got his gun and waited in the parking lot for our victim to arrive.

The new boyfriend, Rolando had no idea that Daniella, who lives in apartment 324 had a boyfriend with a violent past. Alberto had just gotten out of prison three months ago for aggravated battery where he almost killed a man.

Our shooter, Alberto, had put on an old security guard uniform shirt. As Rolando pulled into the parking lot, he was flagged down by Alberto, now looking a lot like a security officer. Alberto was later described a Latin male, 5 feet, 6 inches tall with a full beard and tattoos.

Rolando, seeing the security officer, stopped his car when the officer puts his hand in the air. As Alberto approached the driver's side of the car, he looked around and saw no one. He motioned for the driver to roll down the window. Alberto Mena pulled out a two-inch revolver from his right pocket and pressed it against Rolando's chest and fired twice. The contact wound was deafened by the fact that the other windows were rolled up and the barrel of the gun was pressed against Rolando's chest.

Mena turned and ran as the vehicle rolled forward, still in drive for twenty yards into a parked car. The driver, Rolando was killed when the first bullet pierced his heart.

Several people on the fourth floor witnessed the shooting and called the police. They called it in as a traffic accident. A traffic investigator was dispatched and arrived shortly thereafter. Once on the scene, he knew this was no traffic accident and called Criminal ID and a homicide detective.

I was notified that we had a homicide and responded to the scene. Upon arrival, I observed that the victim was deceased in the front seat of a yellow Camaro. He had been shot twice in the chest. His car was still running. There were no casings at the crime scene. I didn't have much to go on.

One witness came forward and was interviewed. She stated that she saw a Latin male, five feet six or eight inches tall, a full beard, red and blue sneakers, medium build and wearing a security guard shirt. He was talking to the driver-victim before he was shot. She said she didn't see the shooting but thought she may have heard the shots fired. She was not sure if it was gunfire or two cars colliding.

She didn't see the shooting, but she did see that same Latin male wearing the security guard shirt running through the parking lot. That is all she remembered. I thanked her and started working the scene and the vehicle.

After over an hour, the body was still in the vehicle. I didn't want to move it until we had our diagrams, trajectory laser tests, fingerprints, DNA samples and photographs complete. You can never go back and create a crime scene to perfection. You have one shot and you better get it right.

If you work homicide, you'll know that many times the shooter will come back to the scene disguised as a spectator and be extremely curious as to what happened. The shooter wants to find out what the police know and make sure he didn't forget anything or leave evidence behind. So, when I work a homicide scene, I always ask the Criminal ID unit to very discreetly photograph the crowd.

I was standing there, drawing a diagram, when I noticed a Latin male in the crowd. He matched the basic description of the shooter except he was clean shaven. I looked at him and his face was tanned but his jaw, chin and neck were white. Whoever this guy was, he had a beard a long time before shaving today.

I'm thinking, what are the chances the shooter shaved his beard, changed his clothes and came back to the scene? I needed to see his sneakers. I walked outside the ring of spectators and got behind him. Sure enough….his sneakers were red and blue! I asked Detective Ubeda and Alvarez to carefully approach him and ask him if he saw anything.

He said he heard the two gunshots from his apartment that he shares with his girlfriend. Now, he is the only witness who stated that he heard two shots. Most of the residents stated that they didn't hear anything.

After a brief conversation with him, I went to his apartment, #324 to talk to his girlfriend.

When she opened the door, it was apparent that she had been crying. I identified myself and asked if I could enter. She said, "Sure, come on in." I asked her about her boyfriend, Alberto. She stated, "He's not my boyfriend. Just a friend." As I stood near the front door, looking around, I noticed a security guard's shirt draped over a kitchen chair.

I decided to go for the jugular and asked her, "Why did Alberto shave his beard off today?" She replied, "I don't know, you'll have to ask him."

I then raised Ubeda and Alvarez on the radio and told them to '39' the witness, Alberto. 39 meaning, to arrest him. They understood and handcuffed Alberto.

I stayed in the apartment while Detective Ubeda secured a search warrant. In the meantime, Daniella gave me permission to search the apartment. She didn't know that we were detaining Alberto downstairs.

I found the 2-inch revolver he shot Rolando within the closet. I examined the security guard shirt and I could see a fine mist of blood splatter on it. When he shot Rolando from outside the vehicle, there was some blowback that got on the shirt.

We took him into custody without incident. As we were cuffing him, he kept telling us it wasn't him.

After shooting the victim twice in the chest, he went to his apartment, showered, shaved and changed his clothes except for the red and blue sneakers. When I got the search warrant for the apartment, I recovered the firearm and the shirt with blood splatter for evidence. Three months later, he pled guilty and was sentenced to 25 years without chance of parole.

8.12 Are You Really Injured?

This is a story about being on the SWAT Team. I expected more from my team members than just being good police officers. Any officer can work as a uniform patrol officer but to be on the SWAT team or any other specialized unit, takes more than just showing up.

One of the qualities I looked for in a new team member was being smart and also being tough. Can you perform under pressure? If you are shot, can you kill the shooter before you die? Will you stop fighting if you are injured? Most SWAT schools answer a lot of those questions, but only real life-threatening situations will tell me what the man or woman is really made of.

One day, we were shooting our monthly firearms qualification. On this day, we were qualifying with shotguns. Some of the shotguns had cut down stocks and some were full size. The team member had to quality with either shotgun. We were shooting slugs and 9 pellet buck shot. Both rounds produced a pretty good kick when fired.

I was running the line of shooters and they had just finished the shotgun prone position. One of the team members on the line raised his hand and requested permission to come off the line. I walked over to Frank Veteran and told him to stand up and I said, "Why are you requesting to come off the line?" When he stood up and turned around, that is when I could see his face. I was a little bit shocked. Frank must have put the gunstock near his face or did something wrong because the stock of the shotgun came back and hit him in the mouth. He had a large tear in his lip. When he stood up, I asked him, "What in the hell happened to your lip?" He replied, "I don't know sergeant, but the stock hit me in the face."

The blood was gushing out of the one-inch cut on his lip and face. It was running down his chin and soaking his black BDU shirt. Now all of the team members were looking at me and Frank. They were thinking, "What is Sergeant Philbrick going to do?"

I said, "Frank that is a pretty nasty cut on your lip." He replied, "Sir, I can't see it but I think it is because my shirt is soaked with my blood." I then asked him, "Did you finish qualifying?" He said, "No sir, I have two more positions to finish." I said, "When you finish the shotgun qualifications, then you can go to the hospital." He replied, "Roger that,

Sir" and turned back to finish his qualifications. I then looked at the team and they all immediately jumped back in line to finish their qualifications.

Frank finished qualifying and went to the hospital and got six stitches in his lip. We never discussed that night, but I think the team got the message. If you are injured, take care of business and then tell me you are hurt.

Are You Really Injured: Point of Survival

If you are on a SWAT operation and you get shot, before you fall to the ground and die, kill the mother fucker who shot you. In most shootings, you will have three or four seconds to live before you die. This is your opportunity to get even. Don't die alone.

8.13 Poor Me

About six months later, we were practicing rappelling down a forty-story building in the city of Miami. The team was simulating making an entry into a room through a window on the 15th. Floor, firing a shotgun blast into the room and then exiting back out the window and rappelling down to the ground.

I never was a great rappel guy. I just didn't like dangling on ropes 100 feet in the air. Anyway, here I go. I rappelled down about half-way and kicked off the building and released my brake hand on the rope and accelerated down the side of the building really fast. I went a little too fast. When I came back in contact with the building, I hit a metal railing with my left leg. I thought I could get my feet up on time but that didn't happen. When I hit the metal railing, I tore a gash in my left shin about six inches long and about a half inch deep. I completed the rappel and pulled my pant leg up. It was one nasty gash and a very deep cut. I could put my finger in it almost past the top of my fingernail. The pain was incredible. Several of the team members said, "Sarge, you better go to the hospital and get that taken care of." I didn't and I couldn't. I had made Frank finish the shotgun course and I had to stay and finish the rappelling with the team.

We finished about an hour later. By then, my boot was full of blood and the pain was quite severe. Everyone wanted to see the wound. All I heard from team members was, "Suck it up Sarge." To make matters worse, this idiot (that would be me, the author), told the team, "I'll go to the hospital after we finish dinner." So, just to make a point with the team, I went to eat with everyone in a Cuban restaurant. Only after dinner, did I go to the hospital and have my leg looked at.

Fifteen stitches later, I am still one tough son of a bitch, but maybe not the sharpest tool in the shed.

Poor Me: Tactical Point:

Whether you're in SWAT or protecting your family, keep fighting. But the point was made. If you are on SWAT, you had better be tough. But here is the lesson for the person reading this book: If you are fighting for your life, there is a good possibility that you will get injured defending yourself against the attacker. If you are hurt, you have got to work through the pain and injury to survive. When the attack is over, only then can you nurse your wounds. It is not going to be pretty, but if you continue to resist and fight, you can survive. Never give up. Pain and injury are temporary, but death is final.

8.14 Visualization

Many times, as a member of the SWAT team, I had to perform above expectations. I was SWAT and not your regular patrol officer. As a team member, we all received specialized training. I was the team member who carried the sledgehammer or the ram. It was my job to break the door in so the team could make entry. If I failed to perform, the team was in immediate danger because the subjects inside were usually armed. There could be no delay in getting in. Any delay and the subjects inside the house would begin shooting out the front door.

Several times we were told the subject in the house was heavily armed and the door was fortified from the inside. It was my job to stand in front of the door and smash it in. If anyone was to get shot, it would be me. Again, I had to do my job with efficiency and speed. I couldn't have a bad day. If I did, the team would never make it through the door and into the house. We could all get killed. I could not fail.

Just prior to the team arriving at our target location, I would close my eyes and visualize what I was about to do. I would see myself conducting the mission. I would visualize the police SWAT van stopping. I would be yelling to the SWAT team members, "Let's go, go, go!" I would visualize moving the safety on my MP-5 machine gun from on to off, and then the selector switch to semi-automatic or fully automatic. I then saw myself jumping out of the van, running, approaching the front door and yelling, "Police, search warrant, open the door!"

I would then visualize hitting the door with the ram with every muscle in my body. "Door open, door open, go, go, go." I would then throw the 35-pound ram down on the ground, parallel to the wall so I would not hit my team members as they were making entry. As the team makes entry, I have to wait until the number three man enters. The team leader is always the number four man. Entering behind the number three man, I shoulder my MP-5 machine gun with my finger off the trigger.

I'm yelling, "Hialeah Police, search warrant. Everyone, get down!" I would sweep the house for subjects, see a target, determine if he has a gun, decide whether to shoot or not to shoot, yell "Get down, get down, you're under arrest," move to the next room, clear the room, yell, "Secondary search, all clear!" Wow! let's go, I'm ready!

After a few seconds, I would open my eyes and do just what I visualized in my mind. I had just completed the operation to perfection.

Visualization: Teaching Point

Visualization works. It's a proven technique used by Olympic athletes for competition. Just prior to the diver leaving the platform, you can see him mentally and physically going through the dive with his body and mind. He is visualizing the perfect dive, then goes.

For crime prevention, visualize being robbed. Go through the images of what could happen. See it in your mind. Feel it in your body. What would you have to do to survive? Play the scenario out. See yourself doing the right thing to survive.

Visualize being home and see the home invaders break down your front door. What are you going to do? Visualize getting the gun that is stored in the closet. See yourself swiftly arming yourself and moving towards the bedroom to protect your family. The visualization prepares you and gets you in the right mental state. After seeing the scenario in your mind three or four times, say to yourself, "I have done this before and I'm ready."

8.15 Getting Shot or Stabbed

In a gun fight or an armed robbery, the chance of you getting shot is relatively high if you are in close proximity to the shooter. The robber will most likely not aim the gun but just point the gun and pull the trigger. This is called point shooting.

Point shooting is really quite effective. There will be no time for the assailant to aim his weapon. He will point the gun and pull the trigger more than one time.

Most gun fights and armed robberies occur at a very close range. Usually, the scenario will be within four to six feet. The action will be fast and deadly. Getting shot is something you cannot train for.

Gun fights are won on shot placement and not how fast you shoot or how many bullets you fire. Shot placement is where the bullet impacts the human body. What wins gunfights is hitting organs that sustain life. You will most likely not survive if you are shot in the head, spinal cord, chest cavity or a major artery. You will survive if you are shot in the leg, arm, shoulder, etc.

If you are shot, it is paramount that you keep fighting. Even if your bullet wound is lethal and you are going to die, you will have four to six seconds to get even. It is a fact that if you are shot, not in the head, but other organs and you are going to die you will have a few seconds before you die.

It will take everything you have to concentrate and return fire before you drop to the ground dead. If you do nothing after being shot, the subject will close in on you and make sure that you will die. Don't die alone. Return fire, if you can, and take the shooter with you.

If you are in a knife fight, distance is your friend. Create distance between you and the attacker. Keep the subject with the knife away from you and if you can put something between you and the assailant. That could be a chair, suitcase, umbrella or anything that gives you space.

The key to surviving a knife attack is to minimize your cuts to areas on your body that are not life threatening. That would be your hands, top of your forearms, foot, lower leg etc. Most knife attacks can be seen coming if you watch the attacker's hands and his body positioning. The attacker will telegraph the knife attack.

8.16 Dead on top of the Stairs

The call went out as a domestic disturbance. I was the first officer to arrive. As I walked up to the apartment building, everyone was pointing to the top of the stairs. I ran over to the stairs and went up about five steps and stopped. There was a man in his forties sitting on top of the stair landing. He had a deep stab wound to the inside of his left leg. The knife wound had severed his femoral artery.

I told dispatch, "Give me fire rescue on a three reference to a knife wound." I told the man to take his fist and push as hard as he could on the knife wound. With direct pressure, the bleeding might slow down. He was losing a lot of blood and the blood was running down the stairs. I kept talking to him and checked with dispatch that fire rescue was notified. I knew he didn't have long to live. He had lost too much blood. I couldn't administer first aid to him. First, I had to find out who stabbed him and place that person in custody.

I followed the blood trail to apartment #2 on the second floor. Inside the apartment was a young woman in her early twenties. She was holding a bloody 8-inch carving knife. There was blood everywhere.

At gun point, I told her to put the knife down and she did. I holstered my Glock pistol and told her to sit down. I asked her why she stabbed the victim. She stated, "Cheat on me. That will be the last time."

I arrested his wife and was in the process of handcuffing her while another officer was trying to administer first aid to the injured husband. The other officer didn't do a very good job looking after the injured male. After about two minutes, the victim passed out and fell four steps down the stairs to the first step. I put his wife in my car and went back to the stairs just as fire rescue pulled up. He was dead on the scene. He had lost too much blood to survive.

Dead on the Stairs: Medical Point

With a wound that deep, and blood gushing out, only a tourniquet could have saved his life. In that case, seconds counted. My back-up could have saved the man's life. You can't always wait for fire rescue. Today, there are a lot of officers carrying a trauma kit on their outer tactical vest. You can save a life with a trauma kit. Learn how to use it.

8.17 Knife Wound

I was dispatched to a knife fight in a residential housing area. I was third on the scene. When I got there, the other patrol units were handcuffing the subject. He had stabbed a male with a four-inch carpet knife.

I discovered another white male standing in front of the house. His shirt was off and he was holding his right breast with his left hand. He was squeezing his chest and applying pressure to his cut. There was not much blood coming from the wound. I said, "Are you injured?" He replied, "Yea, this guy cut me pretty good with a rug knife."

I quickly called dispatch and verified fire rescue was on route. They were nearby and you could hear them coming. I then turned my attention back to the victim. I couldn't see the wound, so I said, "Where are you cut? Let me see." He then took his left hand off his chest and I saw a deep cut about three inches long. Immediately, his heart pumped out a stream of bright red blood about two feet in the air coming out from the wound. I quickly said, "OK, put your hand back over the cut and press hard." About this time, fire rescue was on scene and I directed them to the victim holding his chest and pinching off the artery.

This was a good example of arterial bleeding and that direct pressure on the wound will slow down the blood flow.

Knife Wound: Medical Point

Learn some self-first aid. You may have to stop the bleeding on yourself or another person until the police or fire rescue arrives. This story shows that if you put direct pressure on a major artery, it will stop bleeding.

8.18 Shooting a Bum

It was just past 11:00 pm on a very cold night in South Florida for the month of January. I was the on-duty Homicide Sergeant. I was driving back to the detective bureau office when the police radio alert tone sounded. There was a long beep tone and dispatch blurted, "Shots fired, subject down at East 11th. Avenue and 8th. Street in the shopping plaza. Fire Rescue on route.

It took me about four minutes to get to the scene of the shooting. Upon arrival, patrol units had sequestered a security guard in uniform off to the side. He had a belt on but no holster. Fire rescue paramedics were standing over the body of an elderly man. He was wearing three shirts and two jackets. There was a large pool of blood on the pavement from a single gunshot wound to his body. He was dead.

The security officer was the one who shot the vagrant and also called the police. On the scene of the shooting, he told me and the patrol officers that the subject was breaking into a vehicle and that's why he shot him. The only problem was, when the security guard called the police from his cell phone, he told dispatch the following: "I just shot a man who was getting into a vehicle. I sneaked up on him and pulled my gun out. When I put the gun to his back and said, 'Security,' he turned, suddenly and the gun went off by accident. I didn't mean to shoot him. I think he's dead. Please come quickly." This entire statement was recorded by police communications.

My investigation revealed that the security guard was not authorized or licensed to carry a firearm. In South Florida, you need to have a 'G Firearms License' to carry a gun in uniform.

The homeless man was cold, looking for a warm place to sleep. He was not a criminal. He was getting into the vehicle to keep warm. The temperature was in the low 40s, which is very cold for Florida. The security officer observed the vagrant trying car doors. He was just looking for a car to sleep in.

When he saw the vagrant, the unarmed and unlicensed security guard went to his car and took his gun out of his glove box and quietly approached the vagrant. The homeless man opened the door to a vehicle and the security guard was right behind him. He put the barrel of the gun in the vagrant's back and yelled, "Security Officer, don't move!" It scared the vagrant so much that he quickly turned around, pushing the gun back into the guard. The guard had his finger on the trigger and pulled it when the vagrant moved so fast.

The bullet penetrated the vagrant's back and exited out his heart, killing him instantly. Immediately after that, the guard called the police and admitted to mistakenly killing the man.

The security guard pled manslaughter and should be out soon.

Legal Point:

If you are ever involved in a shooting or have to use deadly force to defend yourself, be careful what you say. After a life-threatening, traumatic event, people want to talk about it and tell someone. Don't!

When you call the police, do not incriminate yourself. State the facts only. For example, "I've been involved in a shooting. The subject is injured. Send fire rescue to this location." Also, be careful when you talk to witnesses. They can be subpoenaed to testify against you about what you said.

As a homicide investigator, the last person I talk to is the shooter. I'll get all the answers when I come to interview you. You have plenty of time to get your attorney on the phone or have him or her come to the scene. It would be good advice not to talk to anyone until you have spoken to your attorney.

Remember, when a police officer is involved in a shooting, a PBA, or a Police Benevolent Association union representative, or an attorney is dispatched automatically to the scene. Normally, the officer will not give a statement until several days after the shooting.

Shooting someone is a traumatic event. Don't make any statements until your head is clear and you have legal counsel present.

8.19 A Heroic Victim

One evening, I was just getting off duty and about to go home. It was about 1:30 am and a dispatch emergency alert tone sounded on my police radio. The alert tone gets your attention and identifies the call related to a crime in progress or an emergency.

Examples of when a police radio alert tone would be used are when a burglary is in progress, a traffic accident where a car is in a canal, shots have been fired and victims are down, or an officer needs emergency backup.

The alert tone stopped and dispatch stated, "Thirty-three in progress, the subject is armed with a handgun." A '33' is a rape. Dispatch then gave the location and address of the rape in progress. I was not very far from the location. I advised dispatch that I was on route.

Prior to my arrival, this is what had occurred. Rose, a 77-year old woman heard a knock at her front door. She looked out the window and recognized the subject as the same man who had been there last night. She called 811 and said, "There is a man at my door. I've seen him here before. Last night, this same man masturbated on my front door." Dispatch said, "We have officers on the way. Ma'am, what is he doing now?"

Rose then put the phone down on the table and started opening the door. She felt safe because she had five chain locks on her door. The chain locks kept her door from opening not more than three or four inches.

As she was unlocking her dead bolt and opening the door, dispatch was trying to tell her, "Please stay on the phone and do not open your door." She was old and debilitated and used a walker. She also had a gun; a Smith and Wesson revolver in her hand. So, there she was, an elderly female with one hand on the walker and the other hand holding a gun.

Dispatch was still on the line and heard what happened next. The woman cracked the door open about three inches and asked, "What do you want?" The attacker violently kicked in her front door. His kick broke all of the chain locks. When the door flew open, it hit the woman, sending her falling backwards onto the floor. Her walker went flying and she dropped the revolver.

She began screaming as dispatch listened. In a clear voice, Rose yelled out, "He's raping me." Dispatch said, "Subject is inside the apartment, raping the victim." I was still three blocks away, but two patrol officers advised that they were about to arrive on the scene.

The intruder now had her gun and was beating her with the butt of the firearm while he was trying to pull off her panties. Dispatch again sent out an alert tone and stated, "Be advised the subject is armed and is raping the woman." I heard this and raced toward the rape in progress.

The elderly victim, who was extremely smart, put her head and shoulders under a chair and tried to cross her legs. All the while, she knew that the police were listening and she kept yelling, "He's got my gun, get off me. I'm older than your mother. Please stop. He's raping me."

Everyone in the city was hearing this on the police radio. She continued yelling, "Get off me. He's raping me. Get off me!" Then there was nothing but silence on the radio. The subject hit her several times in the head with her gun and knocked her unconscious. Dispatch then asked, "Are you ok?" She didn't respond. Then I heard nothing.

When the officers arrived, the rapist was between her legs and armed with the gun and had beaten her into unconsciousness. When I arrived, the officers were handcuffing the rapist. The victim was unattended.

I watched the officers handcuff the subject and as I turned around to aid the victim, she had already gotten up. Blood was streaming down her face and head. He gun was in her right hand and she was moving closer to her handcuffed attacker. I had to restrain her. It didn't take much to stop her. She said, "Let me shoot him, he raped me, let me shoot him." If I hadn't stopped her, she would have sot the man who had just raped her.

Survival Point:

After her rapist pled guilty and got 15 years in prison, I asked Rose if she wouldn't mind telling her story to a women's group and at rape seminars. She said she would love to.

I taught a few rape prevention seminars and I would place her in the audience and tell the 40 or 50 women there, how she fought back and survived. When I played the audio tape from dispatch, there wasn't a dry eye in the crowd. I would then introduce her to the class so she could tell her story and answer questions. She was one resilient woman. She fought back and survived the brutal attack. She shared her attack so other women could learn from her ordeal and survive.

I am always asked, "Is it good to fight back if attacked by a rapist? The answer is, "First, does he have a weapon and secondly, what is your location." "Is he armed and where are you? If you are in a crowded mall then fight like hell. But, if you are attacked in a vacant lot and no one could hear you if you screamed then that is a totally different scenario.

If you scream can someone hear you? If you run can you find help? If you fight back and are over powered, it could become life threatening. These are all important factors in your attack.

Remember our goal is to survive the ordeal and minimize our injuries.

8.20 I Shot the Good Guy

There is a bar at West 28 Street and 8 Avenue in our jurisdiction. On this night, two Latin males got into an argument inside the bar. They were arguing over a woman. The fight escalated. One of them said, "You know, Hector, I go get a gun and I kill you." He did just that. He went outside and opened the trunk of his Cadillac and took out a 9mm pistol. He concealed the gun in his waistband and went back into the bar.

The argument ensued and the smaller man of the two pulled the 9mm pistol out of his waistband. He got close to Hector and put the gun to his head. At the last minute, Hector grabbed the gun and the firearm discharged just missing his head. Hector yelled, "This guy is trying to kill me. Call the police."

The bullet hit a mirror and the place started emptying. Everyone was running out of the bar including Hector and the shooter. Police dispatched the call as a, "Shooting in progress."

Hector and the subject with the gun were now fighting in front of the bar. The gun went off two more times. Everyone outside was running and diving for cover. Dispatch advised, "Multiple shots being fired."

The first police officer on the scene was Lieutenant Etzler. He got out of his marked vehicle. He drew his .45 caliber semi-automatic pistol, just as Hector wrestled the gun out of the shooter's hand. Now Hector, who is the good guy, thinks he has the situation under control as he turns toward the lieutenant. At the exact same time, Lt. Etzler is yelling, "Drop the gun, drop the gun!" As Hector, the good guy, turns toward the lieutenant showing him he has the gun, he inadvertently pointed the gun in the direction of the lieutenant. The police Lieutenant fired four times striking Hector in the chest with all four rounds. Hector died on the scene minutes later. The police had just killed the good guy.

There was an investigation and the lieutenant was cleared of the shooting. The shooting was ruled a justifiable homicide. Was it a good shooting? The lieutenant did not know who the good guy was or the bad guy. He shot as he was trained to do at the man who pointed the gun at him. Even though it was ruled 'justifiable', the lieutenant did feel terrible about shooting an innocent victim.

I Shot the Good Guy: Deadly Point

The point is, when the police get on scene and you are holding a robber at bay or have a burglar on the ground, do not turn towards the police if you are holding a firearm. Immediately place the gun on the ground, on your vehicle or in your holster.

In all probability, you will be ordered by the responding officers to, "Put the fucking gun down and get on the ground."

As a police officer, I want everyone, and that means everyone on the ground where I can control the scene. Only then, can the officer sort out what happened and decide who the good guys are and who the bad guys are.

Please do as you are told. If you have a rookie police officer who responds to your shooting and you make the wrong move, it could be deadly. Do exactly as the officer tells you and you will live to fight another day.

It comes down to a split second decision. Make it easy on the police and keep your hands up without the firearm.

8.21 Avoiding the Use of Force

It was on the midnight shift in patrol. I was dispatched to a bar fight at the Red Road Lounge. I was the primary unit and a backup officer was also dispatched. When dispatch gave the signal and location, I was about one block away and said, "Show me arriving on the '34' bar fight." A '34' is police terminology for a domestic dispute or a fight.

As I pulled in and exited my vehicle, there he was. It was 'Tree Trunk." That was our nickname for Lenny, one of our community drunks. He was always fighting and creating problems in the city. The problem is that 'Tree Trunk' was about 6'7 and weighed over 300 lbs. Besides being huge, he had tremendous strength and was absolutely crazy. I mean crazy as being nuts! One night, I saw him rip a bumper off a Volkswagen. When you mix being nuts, liquor and muscle all together, there is always going to be a problem.

He was the fight inside the Red Road Lounge and now he was leaving. I stood in front of him and said, in a very firm police authoritative voice, "Lenny, stop and put your hands on the car until I find out what happened inside." He looked at me straight in the eyes and said, "I don't like you. I think I'm going to hurt you." When he said that, he took one step towards me and slowly brought both arms up to grab me.

I looked at him and I took one step back and I'm thinking, I'm 5'10 inches tall, a good 200 plus pounds, current World Police Judo Champion, 5th degree black belt in judo and I teach defensive tactics at the police academy. I'm also wearing a Glock 8mm pistol as my primary duty weapon and I have a .38 caliber, 2-inch revolver on my right ankle. I'm on the SWAT team and all around, I'm one pretty tough son-of-a-bitch! So, I asked myself, "Is he going hurt me?" I'm looking at him and I know he is crazy, and I can arrest him later. I said to myself, "Do I really want fight this guy tonight? Hell no!" I might have won the fight, but not the battle.

No other police officers had arrived. It was just me and 'Tree Trunk.' I quickly looked around and there was no one watching us. As he reached for me again, I backed up and ran to the other side of my police car. He was trying to get me but I kept running around the car so he couldn't catch me. He went one direction and I went the opposite around my car. I kept running with him chasing me for about 25 seconds and finally, he stopped and looked at me and said, "Stop running."

From the other side of the police car, I said, "Lenny, I don't want to hurt you, I am your friend." Meanwhile, I was praying that the backup officer didn't arrive and no one from the bar had seen Lenny chasing Officer Philbrick around his police car. I would not have been more embarrassed. But, I thought, it was better to run now and fight another day.

When I said to him, "Lenny, I don't want to hurt you, I am your friend," he stopped and looked at me and said, "Ants are my friends too." He then turned around and walked away northbound on Red Road.

Now, what are my options? Do I physically engage him, run up and tackle him from the rear or hit him with my baton? Do you know what I did? I quickly cancelled the other unit, got in my car and drove away. As I left the scene, I prayed that no one in the bar saw him chasing me. Yes, it happened just as I described it. Funny, but really embarrassing.

Avoiding Use of Force: Tactical Point

The moral of the story is: If you can avoid a fight, do so. You may be right in the end, but sometimes discretion is more important than valor. He left the bar and I went home that night in one piece. Mission accomplished.

8.22 Verbal Judo

I was dispatched to a domestic argument between a husband and a wife. Upon arrival, I found the two combatants in the front yard and she was throwing all of his clothes out of the house, into the street. His wife had just found out that her husband was cheating on her.

The last thing this husband needed was for a police officer to come into his house and tell him what to do.

As I approached the husband, he turned and looked at me. He immediately took a boxer stance and started clenching his fists. His hands were down by his sides and he took a bladed position, much like the boxer. He then looked right through me as if I wasn't even there.

I tried to keep my distance and told him, "Sir, I need you to step over here and talk to me." When I said that, I could see that he was just waiting for me to get within arm's reach of him so he could swing at me. I knew I was in trouble.

Normally, when police officers are dispatched to a domestic dispute, we arrive and ask, "What's the problem here?" and start ordering the argumentative couple to separate. Not this time. I knew if I did that, this guy was going to be on me.

I kept my distance from the husband. I really didn't want to hurt him or have to take him to jail. I knew his life had just taken a turn for the worse. His wife just found out that he was cheating on her with her best friend. Today was probably one of the darkest days of her life and his. He wasn't angry at me. I knew I had to be careful but at the same time, empathetic.

Rather than issue commands, I said to him, "Sir, I know that you are having a very bad day and I really don't want to make it any worse. But, at this moment, I could use your cooperation and try to resolve this situation.

In the police academy, we are trained to deal with verbal and physical altercations. One tool we are taught is called Verbal Judo; using words to deflect a physical fight. Using a series of words absolutely changes the demeanor of the subject and the police usually gain cooperation from the combatant.

Verbal judo teaches you to gain voluntary compliance from the combatant. One of the best phrases in the art of persuasion is, "What can I do or say to gain your cooperation at this time?" That phrase has worked miracles in my thirty years of police work. Another phrase is, "Sir, would you please come over here and tell me your side of the story." This is called Verbal Judo and it works like magic.

Now, back to the domestic dispute. There was no fight but there would have been if I had been aggressive and failed to use dialogue that was non-threatening and at the same time, showed him some respect. Try it. I think you may find it extremely effective.

Verbal Judo: Teaching Point

If you can, talk your way out of an altercation. It is better than fighting. If you get into a physical brawl, you or the other person could be seriously injured. Verbal judo works, try using it.

8.23 The Loco Cuban

When I was the Detective Sergeant in homicide, I handled an interesting case. Jose, who was Puerto Rican, sold a used car to Pedro, also known as the "Loco Cuban." As luck would have it, the vehicle broke down. Pedro, who bought the car, was known to always carry a firearm and was a little crazy. When the car broke down, he wanted his money back. He called Jose on the phone and said, "You don't give me my money back, I'll kill you."

Jose, knowing that Pedro was crazy and always carried a gun, thought he was justified in killing Pedro first, before Pedro killed him.

Jose got into his car and drove over to the loco Cuban's house and knocked on his front door. When Pedro opened the door, Jose shot him four times in the chest with a .357 Magnum revolver. He died a few minutes later. Jose said, "There, I killed you first."

When I arrived with my homicide team, I interviewed the shooter and asked him what happened. He said, "Sergeant, you know Pedro is crazy and always carries a gun. I sold him a car, but it broke down. That's not my fault. He wanted his money back and I told him, No." He then told me on the phone, "You don't give me my money back, and I'll kill you." I know him, he's crazy and I was afraid he would kill me, so I drove over to his house and I killed him first."

Jose thought he was justified in killing the crazy Cuban first before he killed him first. Was his life in immediate danger? The answer is no. I arrested Jose for second-degree murder. He was sentenced to 15 years in prison.

The Loco Cuban: Legal Point

Don't take the law into your own hands. No one can kill you over the phone. Call the police.

8.24 The Barber

I received a call from the city of Miami Police Department. They were in our jurisdiction watching an apartment where the wife of a homicide subject lived. They were there to see if he would show up at his home. He was wanted on several murders in New Jersey.

At about 2:00 pm, the detectives called the Hialeah Police and said the subject just arrived at his wife's apartment. I drove to the location and met with my captain, lieutenant and the city of Miami detectives. They wanted the SWAT team to enter the apartment and arrest the homicide subject from New Jersey.

Our SWAT Commander advised me to call out the SWAT team from home. I called dispatch and asked for ten SWAT team members to come to my location. They arrived in about 45 minutes and we set up a staging area about one block away.

While the team was suiting up, I had a good visual of the apartment on the second floor. I could see the apartment and the subject's wife was cutting one of the children's hair just outside the open apartment door. There were also two small children playing near the front door of the apartment where the homicide subject was. The chances of a gunfight were good and we didn't want any of the children to get killed or injured.

The plan was to send a female detective in plain clothes up the stairs three seconds before the six-man SWAT team assaulted the apartment. Detective Laura Lefebvre agreed to do this. The entry team would be delayed three seconds before making entry up the stairs and into the apartment. We were concealed at the bottom of the stairs. From the second floor, the homicide subject couldn't see us until we got to the second level stairwell.

The plan was that once Detective Lefebvre got to the second-floor landing, she was to move the children away from the front door in the event of a gunfight. This would also clear a path for the SWAT team to rapidly enter the apartment. I told Detective Lefebvre she had three seconds and to move fast. Everything was a "go" at the bottom of the stairs.

I told her to 'Go!' as the team and I stacked on the first floor of the apartment complex. Wearing a police windbreaker and a bullet proof vest, she started up the stairs. I slowly counted one, two, three and the team quickly moved up the stairs. As we got to the landing on the second floor, the first three SWAT team members saw the subject in the apartment and moved toward the open front door. I was fourth up the stairs. I was yelling, "Police, get down!" as I got to the top of the stairs. The female detective was moving the children to the side when the wife, who was cutting hair, attacked Detective Laura with a pair of six-inch scissors.

She turned with lightning speed and stabbed the detective in the right side of her neck, just missing a major artery. Detective Laura grabbed the wife to restrain her as the wife was coming down to stab her again. She grabbed the detective by the hair and leaned over and bit her on the right cheek. Blood was now gushing out of the bite would as the 'barber' was biting down harder and was about to stab Detective Laura a second time.

The medical doctor who later examined the detective at the hospital, stated that another deep cut from the scissors could have severed her main artery, and also punctured her lung.

At the same time, I was about to enter the apartment, I saw the 'barber' about to stab Detective Laura again. I had not seen her stab her the first time. I moved with amazing speed for an old guy. I caught the 'barber's' right hand half-way down before she could stab the detective again. I had my Glock pistol in my right hand and her wrist with the bloody scissors in my left.

In an attempt to disarm the 'barber,' I slammed her wrist against the meal railing in front of the apartment. She didn't drop the scissors. Detective Laura was screaming, "Get this bitch off me, get her off me!" Remember, that the 'barber' had already stabbed Detective Lefebvre once and was now biting her face and not letting go. She was engaged with the subject and was bleeding from her neck and face at the same time.

I put my Glock 9mm against the 'barber's' head and began to squeeze the trigger, but the detective moved just before I pulled the trigger. I was concerned the bullet might pass through the 'barber's' head and hit the detective who she was still biting. Detective Lefebvre was now yelling, "Shoot her, shoot her. Get her off me. Get the bitch off me!" I tried again but I couldn't get a clear shot. I put my gun back in my holster.

With two hands free now, I slammed the 'barber's' hand again against the metal railing and pried the scissors out of her hand and they fell to the first floor. I then stopped the detective from moving by grabbing the 'barber's hair and controlling her. Finally, I had both women in front of me. Detective Lefebvre was screaming. This entire event was now about ten to twelve seconds in duration.

With the 'barber' stabilized and still chomping down on the detective's right cheek, I used a pressure point on the neck of the 'barber' to finally dislodge her mouth and teeth off of the detective's face. Due to the pain from the pressure point she opened her mouth and I threw her to the ground.

When I finally separated the detective and the 'barber,' I saw the bite wound. You could see the outline of her teeth on the detective's jaw. There was a heavy stream of blood running down the detective's face. She had a deep bite wound on her cheek.

After I threw the 'barber' down, Detective Laura, with two quick strikes stopped the subject from getting up and handcuffed her.

After Detective Lefebvre secured the female, I went into the apartment. The entry team was handcuffing the homicide subject from New Jersey. Mission accomplished.

The Barber: How much force is enough?

This story is about the use of force. Someone with a pair of scissors can kill you. These are called environmental weapons. It could be a metal pen, an iron, a hammer or even a screwdriver. Someone biting you is aggravated battery, which is a felony. You can't shoot someone for biting you but if they have a knife or a pair of scissors and are stabbing you, your life is certainly in danger.

Detective Laura Lefebvre sustained deep scarring and teeth marks on her cheek that are still visible today. She quit police work a few years after this incident. She did buy me a gold medallion and chain with her unit number on the back and thanked me for saving her life.

8.25 The Case of the TV Homicide

I investigated this case when I was assigned to homicide as a sergeant. This is a case of justifiable homicide. Every death is a homicide. Some are justified and some are not. In this case, the girlfriend shot her unarmed boyfriend.

The victim (deceased) was in a biker gang and he and his girlfriend lived together. On the last day of his life, they were arguing in their apartment. As usual, the boyfriend always escalated the argument and it became louder and he punched her in the face. On this day, he became more aggressive and started beating her. He had beaten her twice before and each time she ended up in the hospital.

After he punched her twice, she ran into the bedroom and he followed her. The last time he punched her and beat her up, she was in the hospital for three days. This time, she decided this was not going to happen again.

In the bedroom, he struck her again as she stood next to the bed. She reached in the nightstand and got his gun and told him, "Get back or I'll shoot."

In response to her grabbing his gun, he picked up a portable television that weighed about forty pounds. He had backed her into a corner of the bedroom and he raised the television set above his head and was about to throw it at her. She shot him twice in the chest. One of the bullets pierced his heart. He dropped the TV and died instantly. She had just shot an unarmed man.

As the lead investigator, I did not arrest her. There were several reasons why. First, her boyfriend weighed over 240 pounds and she weighed only 112. He was considerably larger and stronger than she was. Secondly, she told me, after being in the hospital several times, she wasn't going back again. It had to stop.

But, most importantly, were her answers to my questions. I asked her, "Why did you shoot him?" She told me, "I believed my life was in danger. If he hit me on the head with the television, I would be in the hospital again or he could have even killed me this time."

What is interesting about this case is that she only shot him when he put the television above his head to hit her with it. This was proven by the medical examiner. If you raise both your arms above your head, it also raises your rib cage. If you lower your arms, the rib cage slides back over your vital organs.

The medical doctor, at the pretrial hearing showed me and the judge where the two bullets fired never pierced his rib cage even though he was shot in the chest because he had his arms up over his head, holding the television. When he put the TV above his head, it raised his rib cage above most of the organs. But, when he lowered his arms, the cage actually covered both gunshot entry wounds. This physical evidence proved her story that he had his arms raised above his head and was about to smash the TV on top of her head. If she had not shot him, there was a good chance the TV set could have killed her. This case was ruled a justifiable homicide.

The Case of the TV Homicide: Investigative Point

Don't rush to judgement. Before you make your decision, gather all the facts and listen to what the victim or shooter has to tell you. Remember, we interview the primary suspect last. When I interview that suspect, I already have all the answers. Compare the facts to her statement and you just might end up with the truth.

8.26 The Transvestite and the Cop

Detective Kent Hart and I were working vice and narcotics late one night. We both were in plain clothes and in an unmarked civilian car. We were driving up and down Okeechobee Boulevard looking for drug dealers or prostitutes. It didn't matter to us. We could buy drugs and make the arrest or take some hooker off the street. Both were statistics and that's what our unit needed for the month. Arrests were down, so we needed to go out and get some.

That's when I saw a prostitute in front of one of Hialeah's rent by the hour hotels. This hotel charges, not by the day, but by the hour. You pay $25 for an hour and a half. She was a rather large woman, trying to flag down cars with a single male inside.

I was driving and pulled up to her and stopped. She walked over to the car. She was a big girl. I rolled down the window and said, "Where's the party?" That's when she said in a very husky voice, "What are you looking for?"

To arrest a prostitute, you have to get them to solicit you. You cannot entrap them. They have to say something like, "Twenty dollars for sex." This prostitute knew the word game. When she said that to me, "What are you looking for?" I replied, "My friend and I are looking for a little pussy." (I believe I was still within the confines of the law and it was not considered entrapment.) When I said that, she pulled up her dress and showed me her vagina and said, "Does this look like a little pussy?" It was dark, but from her quick flash, it looked like a pussy. She wasn't wearing any underwear.

Kent started laughing and said, "That is not a little pussy." Just when he said that, she reached in the open window and grabbed my groin and squeezed my penis. As she turned and walked away, she said, "Have a nice night, officers."

I looked at Detective Hart and said, "Kent, didn't she just commit battery on a police officer?" (Battery is unlawful touching). He said, "Yea, I think so." I said, "Let's go get her." We both got out of the car to arrest her.

By now, she was half-way to her room. As she walked in the room and tried to close the door. I pushed the door open and yelled, "Police Officer, put your hands behind your back, you are under arrest."

This prostitute was about six feet in height and weighed a good 220 pounds. She was a pretty big girl. When I yelled, "Police Officer, put your hands behind your back," she took a fighting stance. Kent, who was one step in front of me immediately punched her on the left side of her neck. In police work, this strike is called a brachial stun. It was so quick, I said, "Dam, Kent, I think you killed her."

Down went the prostitute on the bed. After Kent hit her, she was totally unconscious and fell face down. When she hit the bed, her dress came up and exposed her buttocks and…..there it was. I could not believe my eyes. I saw a penis and a set of testicles; a very large penis, tied up with a string between his legs. She, excuse me, he had tied a string around the head of his penis and around his testicles and pulled it through his legs and tied it to a string around his waist.

When I was in the car, she/he flashed me. From the front, it looked like a pussy, but in reality, it was a dick and a set of balls strapped to his ass. This was the first time I'd ever seen something like this.

I quickly handcuffed him and seconds later, he woke up. His name was Omar. Omar, the want-to-be transvestite prostitute was subdued by a very quick and effective punch to the neck by Hart. This is not the end to the story.

At the jail, I asked Omar the reason why he pulled his penis through his legs and tied it off. Omar told me, "It looks like a pussy and feels like a pussy to them." He said that he usually gives Male John's head for $25. The male, getting the blow job thinks this girl is blowing him, but in reality, it's Omar, trying to save up enough money for a sex change.

The Transvestite and the Cop: Point of Contact

Make sure you know what you're are paying for. If it looks too good or too easy, it's a scam. Save your money.

8.27 Foot Chase to the Wire

There is an area in our jurisdiction that has sold crack for fifteen to twenty years. It's still being sold in the area but on a much smaller scale.

SWAT-TAC, our narcotics and crime prevention team, would spend hours in Seminola, trying to arrest the dealers, sellers or buyers.

Many times, we would pull up and jump out, pat sellers down, find the drugs and take them to jail. They knew the routine and it turned into a cat and mouse game every time we pulled up, jumped out and chased them. On this night, they were expecting us.

Jim Poole was driving and as soon as we arrived, one of the subjects looked at me and threw something into a 50-gallon drum that was being used as a barbeque and took off running. The fire burns up the crack.

I bailed out of the car and almost caught him as he jumped over a fence. It was dark and I couldn't see ten feet in front of the house. I was, maybe twenty-five feet behind him as he quickly turned left on foot around the house. When he turned the corner, I didn't see him duck and I kept running. He and his friends had tied a wire from the clothesline pole to a tree. It was designed to stop me or one of my guys from catching him. It did.

I was focused on him and not on what was in front of me. In my right hand was my Glock pistol and left hand, a flashlight. I hit the wire neck and chest high. The wire gave just enough to sling shot me backwards about four feet in the air. I hit the ground hard and didn't get up for a while.

The subject I was chasing stopped and started to walk back to where I was. He said, "That's pay-back for all the money you have cost us here in Seminola." I was in a lot of pain and pointed my gun at him and said, "You're under arrest, mother fucker." He just turned and ran.

From that day forward, whenever I gave foot chase, I made damn sure I wasn't running into another wire. Mark one up for the bad guys.

Foot Chase to the Wire: Tactical View

If you are a police officer, make sure you know the person you are chasing doesn't lead you down the wrong road. Many times the subject will stop and position himself or herself to attack the pursuing police officer or like my case, run a wire across the clothesline and lead the pursuing officer to the booby-trap.

The key is to not lose sight of the person you are chasing. After a few hundred yards he will get tired and make his/her apprehension possible. Again, the most important aspect is never give up. Keep chasing your subject until he/she gets tired.

8.28 The Sexy Dog

We were on the midnight shift, working burglaries in the warehouses. I was riding with Bill Connors, a seasoned officer who ran a boxing gym. It was my first week as a police officer and everything was new and interesting.

I was driving southbound on NW 37th. Avenue as we passed NW 57th. Street. NW 37th. Avenue separated Hialeah from Miami Dade County. It was all warehouses, and nobody should be in that area after dark.

As we passed 57th, Officer Connors, my FTO says, "Did you see the car parked down the alley?" I didn't see anything and said, "Do you want to check it out?" Connors replied, "Turn around and let's see why they are parked there." I turned around and drove back and turned into the alley and there it was; a four door Mercury parked facing the railroad tracks. The area was dark and without street- lights. Every stop or police action could be dangerous.

Connors said, "Hit the blues and give them a chance to get dressed." I turned on our rotating emergency lights and saw movement in the vehicle. The Mercury was facing away from us. Most of the time it's a couple or two lovers in the vehicle.

After a minute or so, Connors and I approached the parked car. I took the passenger side while Connors walked up to the driver's door. I turned on my flashlight and lit up the interior of the front seat. There was a dog and a man in the front seat. The male was in his late 50's and was pulling up his pants.

I heard Connors order the driver out of the car. "Get out of the car and put your hands on the hood of your vehicle." I really didn't know what we had rolled up on, but Bill Connors did. The driver was standing in front of both of us. Connors bluntly stated to the male driver, "You're a sick fuck. What if I called your wife?" When Bill said that, the subject stated, "Please don't do that." And started vomiting next to his front wheel.

I looked in the interior of the vehicle and observed the dog's head and neck were tied with a rope to the arm rest of the passenger door. The dog was about fifty pounds, spotted and brown in color. There was a towel draped over the seat and next to the towel on the seat was a jar of lubrication. I walked around the vehicle and noticed the dog's ass had this lube all over it and on his tail and legs. He was fucking the dog.

After observing the dog's butt, Connors said to the male, "You're under arrest for cruelty to animals" as he handcuffed him.

Connors and I then walked the 'Dog Fucker,' as Bill called him, back to our patrol car and placed him in the rear back seat cage.

As we both walked back to impound the Mercury, I said to Officer Connors, "Bill, how could that guy fuck that dog?"

Connors with a sincere and honest reply said, "I don't know, but I know one thing." I'm waiting for words of wisdom from my seasoned Field Training Officer when Bill Connors says, "That dog sure was ugly."

The Sexy Dog: Point

When you are a police officer you see it all. When you're a civilian, it's there, but you just don't see it.

8.29 Kick in the Groin

On this night, we were assigned to seek and find burglars in the warehouse district. Frank, my partner and I were riding two-man. Both of us in plain clothes in a piece of crap vehicle.

There had been a rash of burglaries lately. It must have been around 2am. My partner, Frank Estevez, was a reserve police officer. He had to ride a certain amount of days to keep his police certification active.

Frank was from Cuba and spoke fluent Spanish and average English. Remember, in the 1880's, South Florida endured the Mariel Boat Lift from Cuba. Thousands of refugees were arriving in boats, inner tubes and homemade sail boats. Fidel Castro emptied his jails and the prisoner all came to South Florida. None of them spoke a word of English. I was learning Spanish, but more commands than general conversation.

Sandy Flutie, another police officer, was walking the railroad tracks near NW 62nd. Street. He had his flashlight out and was checking the warehouses for holes in the walls as he worked his way northbound along the tracks. In the past month, a group of commercial burglars were breaking holes in the walls of businesses and warehouses and cleaning them out.

Frank and I were paralleling officer Flutie on NW 37th. Avenue. We would always raise him on the radio and ask him what street he was on. I wanted to be close in the event he discovered something or was in trouble.

As Sandy walked the tracks, he saw a man in front of him about 50 yards north of his location. The man was waving his arms and saying something in Spanish along the lines of "No, turn the flashlight off, here we are." What was occurring was the man was a burglar and he and a group of men had broken a four-foot hole in the back of a clothing warehouse with sledgehammers.

They had piled about half of the contents, (jackets, dress shirts, shoes, ties, etc.), of the warehouse on the ground by the hole.

They were waiting for their buddy in a van to come and pick them up. For a moment, they thought Sandy, in plain clothes was their contact. After a few seconds, Officer Flutie realized what he had found. He quickly radioed me and Frank. I heard him on the police radio. He said, "Burglary in progress, the tracks at 62nd. Street." We were about a half a block away and arrived almost immediately.

By now, all of the burglars were running. It looked like cockroaches when you turn the lights on. There must have been six to eight subjects running in all directions.

I saw that Sandy pulled out his .45 caliber semiautomatic pistol and ordered the man that was waving his arms to the ground. The man put his hands up and laid down on the railroad tracks. We later learned his name was Andre. We handcuffed him and Frank and I chased the other two guys, but we lost them. Out of a group of six to eight burglars, we had one and patrol caught one. Not a very good job of police work. We caught only two of the eight burglars.

I tried interviewing the subjects, but they only spoke Spanish. I asked Frank, to talk to them. I said to Frank, "Tell Andre that if he doesn't tell me who his partners are, I am going to kick him in the nuts." I was only kidding. I never in my police career hit a subject who was handcuffed. I was more professional than that. But at the time, it sounded pretty good.

Frank walked over to where Andre was standing. Andre was cuffed and stood right in front of Frank. I expected Frank to go over and talk to him. Frank went over to Andre and stood directly in front of him and kicked him in the groin as hard as he could. I immediately said, "Frank, what the hell are you doing?" Frank said, "I thought you told me to kick him in the nuts." I was stunned. "Frank"', I said, "I thought you spoke better English than that. I just meant to scare him. I didn't want you to actually kick him in the nuts. I told you, if he didn't tell us where the other burglars were, I would kick him in the nuts."

Now, Andre was puking and doubled over on the ground. I really felt terrible and I picked him up and sat him down on a milk crate. I went to my car and got a bag with ice and gave it to him. Later, I apologized to him for the misunderstanding. He was ok with it. Being from the prisons in Cuba, he said, "This is normal treatment of prisoners in most jails in my country." I told him, "Not in mine and I am so sorry."

Does a kick to the groin work? Absolutely, just ask Andre. We ended up arresting Andre again four months later on another commercial warehouse burglary. That time, he used a torch and cut the door in half, leaving the alarm intact, but gaining entry into the warehouse. We were better this time. We caught him, and four of his fellow burglars. You know what's funny? He puked again, but this time, he was just scared. Sandy nicknamed him, "Andre, the Puke." So much for the justice system.

Kick in the Groin: Teaching Point

Burglars are good at what they do. Some use different methods to break in and steal your property. Don't underestimate them. They are professionals and are very creative in breaking into your house or business. Always have secondary alarms inside. Protect what you own, or you won't have it very long.

8.30 The Speed of a Knife Attack

The Hialeah Police SWAT team was dispatched to an apartment where an armed and barricaded subject had threatened to kill his mother and responding police officers. The mother called the police after fleeing the apartment. Her son had a history of mental problems and was in the apartment alone.

Patrol officers set up a perimeter around his apartment. He was refusing to come out. This is called a barricaded subject. The mother stated that her son, age 28, did not have a firearm but had a collection of knives and had threatened her before with a knife.

I was home when I got the call to respond to the barricaded subject. When I arrived on the scene, six of our SWAT personnel were positioned outside the apartment door in the hallway. At the same time, police negotiators were attempting to talk the subject out from just outside his closed apartment door. He was inside the apartment talking from behind the closed front door.

I warned fire rescue personnel and the SWAT negotiators to move back from the apartment because they were just too close. They were positioned in the hallway, not more than ten to twelve feet from the subject's door.

He was talking with the negotiators every four to five minutes. It looked like it was going to be a long night. Every once in a while, the subject would take a knife and run it along the bottom of the closed door, exposing the blade to the officers in the hallway. I remembered thinking that his behavior was a little crazy.

Our SWAT Lieutenant, J. Elizarde, arrived on the scene and took command. The six SWAT personnel, two negotiators, and fire rescue were approximately ten to twelve feet from the front door of the apartment. Fire rescue personnel were sitting on top of their equipment, bored out of their minds. They had all moved closer to the door after I had moved them back for better communications.

Meanwhile, the police negotiators were talking to the subject. They told him if he didn't come out, the SWAT team would deploy tear gas into the apartment and force him out. As they were negotiating with the barricaded individual through the door, he suddenly stopped talking. There was only silence. This lasted about two minutes. The SWAT team and negotiators moved closer so they could continue negotiating with him. They were knocking on the door, trying to get him to continue communications. Sgt. Beyer and Kent Hart were also close to the door. They were there to protect the negotiator.

Without warning, the subject, armed with a ten-inch butcher knife, opened the apartment door and in a flash, was in the hallway. He immediately attacked the SWAT team officers protecting the negotiators. In less than two seconds, he had opened the door, run out into the hallway and covered the ten feet where the negotiators and SWAT personnel were standing.

The subject was holding the razor sharp, ten-inch kitchen knife in his right hand. He slashed at SWAT team leader, Sgt. Ed Beyer and cut his vest from top to bottom. He then quickly turned to cut another SWAT team officer and attacked him next. The attacker lunged at Kent Hart and slashed at him with the knife, cutting his ballistic vest also, but not the officer.

A bullet proof vest is no match for a sharp knife. Both officers were thankful they had the tactical vests on top of the ballistic vest. It saved their lives. The subject cut both tactical vests from top to bottom.

After he had attacked the SWAT team officer, both officers opened fire with their MP-5 machine guns as he moved toward the two negotiators. He was hit six times, killing him. It was unfortunate that we were called to save a life and ended up taking a life instead. In reality, it was his choice.

The Speed of a Knife Attack: Tactical Point

In SWAT missions, people barricade themselves in their houses or apartments for many reasons. Sometimes, they have a hostage and other times, they are mentally unstable, or they are just wanted by the police. Regardless, it is dangerous for the police to forcibly enter the dwelling. Tactically speaking, it might be better to gas him out rather than force him out by making entry. Safety of the team is paramount.

8.31 Car in the Canal

In February, in South Florida, the weather is a little chilly. It was about 2:30am. I'd been riding by myself on midnights for about two months. Still a Rookie, but learning fast. Dispatch sounded the alert tone for a crime or emergency in progress.

A female dispatcher slowly said, "Attention 2112 and 2115. Car in canal. Okeechobee and SE 8th. Avenue." I was unit 2115 and I advised dispatch that I was at SE 2nd. Avenue and Okeechobee Road.

I arrived about one minute later to see a submerged, dark colored Chevrolet. The only part of the vehicle visible was the rear bumper and taillights.

I could see where the vehicle drove off Okeechobee Road into the canal. There was nobody on the bank or in the water. The driver must be trapped in the vehicle. As fast as I could, I took off my bullet proof vest, shoes and police leather with my firearm in it and dove into the canal.

I surfed for over twenty years. I'm not a bad swimmer. I hit the cold dark water and swam to the vehicle. I got to the partially submerged vehicle after about twenty strokes. It was dark and I couldn't see inside the vehicle from the surface.

By now, other police units were arriving. I took a deep breath and went under water as I felt my way to the driver's door. It was not locked. I opened the door, opened my eyes and reached in to grab the driver or anybody sitting in the driver's seat. I could see about two feet in front of my face. There was no one in the driver's seat.

Now, I was afraid the car would sink, taking me down with it if the air bubble in the trunk ran out of air. I came up for air and went back down trying to reach across the driver's seat to the passenger's seat. There was no one there. By now, Officer Dennis Kerrigan was in the water with me and I told him to check the back seat. He said, "I already did, QRU." Which meant, everything was ok.

We both swam back to the bank while the car slowly sank out of sight. You could still see the lights on in the car at the bottom of the canal. It wasn't very deep.

Fire rescue gave us blankets to dry off and stay warm. About that time,

Karl Weber walked over and said to me, "Hey, Rookie, don't you know a 22 from a real traffic accident?"

Weber said, 'Rookie, do you see any brake skid marks or another vehicle that forced the car into the canal?"

A little confused, I said, "No, I didn't see any skid marks."

He said, "When they pull the car out of the canal, there should be a concrete brick on the gas pedal. Someone was just dumping a stolen vehicle."

I looked at Kerrigan and he didn't say anything. Then Weber said, "You went into the water for nothing. You'll learn, Rookie."

Kerrigan and I had to go to the hospital due to the infectious materials in the canal. They pulled the car out of the canal and there was a large concrete block on the gas pedal.

Car in the Canal: Tactical Point

I felt a little stupid, but I would do it again. Next time, there might be a family in the car and not a piece of concrete. You wouldn't know until you get in the water and check out the interior of the submerged vehicle.

I'm going in every time. That is my job.

8.32 Man with a Knife

I had just left the station and was on route to court when a 332 in progress went out. A 332 is police code for a fight in progress and someone is dead or injured. Dispatch stated, "Two men fighting with knives." I was three blocks away from the knife fight and I arrived less than a minute later. I got on the radio and said, "Dispatch, show me arriving."

I pulled up in my patrol car and exited my vehicle. I was in my full police uniform for court. I saw two men with knives. I yelled, "Drop the knives." One of them was bleeding on his arm with an obvious knife wound. I looked behind me and realized that I was the only officer there. No one else had arrived. I looked in my right hand and I had instinctively drawn my Glock 19 semi-automatic pistol out of my holster.

I pointed my gun at both men and commanded them to drop their knives. One male subject dropped the knife and put his hands in the air and said in broken English, "No shoot, no shoot!" The other subject, holding the marine style boot knife looked at me and pointed the knife in my direction. Like, "come on!" I couldn't believe what he was doing. The entire ordeal was now about ten seconds long.

I'm about twelve feet from the armed subject and I looked at him and I said to myself, "Do I really want to shoot this stupid son of a bitch?" He looked about sixty years old and appeared possibly drunk. Now, we were fifteen seconds into the knife fight.

To my right, a lady screamed something in Spanish, "No, No," and then "Police stop!" The male was now about eight feet in front of me and he actually jabbed at me with the knife, like "get back."

At the same time, another woman was screaming, "No, Poppy, no!" as I gently pulled back the trigger on my Glock 9mm pistol. I said to myself, "I'm going to shoot him twice if he lunges at me again or gets any closer. We circled each other like two roosters, looking for the opening to attack.

In an instant, I moved forward and kicked this man in the chest as hard as I could. He flew backwards and hit a car behind him, dropped the knife and fell to the ground. I moved in and immediately handcuffed him. I arrested him for aggravated assault on a police officer. The other subject went to jail in another police car for disorderly conduct.

Now, could I have shot this old man, who was intoxicated? Yes, I could have. Would it have been a good shooting? Absolutely. Would I have felt good about shooting him? The answer was 'no.' I had skills (judo and some karate) that aided me from using deadly force. You can be justified in a shooting, but in the end, you have to live with the outcome. I would have felt bad.

I saved a life today by changing my mind.

Man with a Knife: Tactical Point

You have choices every day. Before you take a life, quickly measure your options and make the best decision. You will not have much time. React quickly.

8.33 Man with a Gun

This happened late one night in the early 80's before everyone had a gun. I was assigned to a plain clothes unit and driving an unmarked car. We were working midnight robberies of convenient stores.

I pulled up to the intersection of East 8th. Avenue and 25th. Street. I looked to my left and there was a Ford Mustang next to me with tinted windows. The driver looked at me and then leaned over and picked something up. It was late at night and the windows were tinted but I know what I observed. He looked at me and picked a gun up off the seat and showed it to me. He put it next to his face and maybe blew the gun like a gunslinger would do.

Again, he was holding what looked like a gun, kind of like he was saying, "Look at this mother fucker." His windows were tinted and my visual was not 100%. I couldn't tell if it was a revolver or a semi-automatic.

I let him pull forward and I raised dispatch, "I have a man with a gun at East 8th. Avenue and 25th. Street. He is driving a black Ford with tinted windows, eastbound. I need a marked unit to stop the driver." A marked unit, about a quarter mile away arrived in less than a minute. The uniformed police officer got behind the Ford, activated his emergency lights and we conducted a felony stop on the man with the gun.

I was thinking, the best charge I may have is a felony for carrying a firearm and unlawful display of a firearm. The marked unit, knowing the driver had a gun, used his PA system to get the driver out of the car. On the vehicle's public address system (Megaphone), he said, "Driver, exit the vehicle with your hands high in the air. Do not touch the firearm in the car." The driver complied but when he got out, he said, "I don't have a gun."

The patrol officer then told the driver, "Put both of your hands on the trunk of your car facing away from me." The driver complied with his commands, but all the time kept saying, "What gun are you talking about?" We cuffed him and searched the car for the firearm. I know what I saw; he had a gun in his hand!

The patrol officer could not find the gun. So, I said, "Let me search his car." I searched the entire vehicle and could not find the gun either. I asked the driver, "Where is the gun you had in your right hand?" He replied, "I saw you next to me at the traffic light. I was eating a piece of chicken. Look on the passenger seat and you will find a KFC (Kentucky Fried Chicken) box. I went into his vehicle and grabbed the KFC box and pulled out a crispy fried chicken wing and thigh that looked just like a gun…at night… tinted windows…and in someone's hand; I could not believe my eyes. Did I actually mistake this big piece of chicken in his hand for a gun?

I quickly un-cuffed the driver, wiped him off and apologized to him for several minutes and tried to get the uniform patrol officer to clear as soon as possible. The patrol officer was laughing hysterically. The man with the gun, I mean chicken leg was very understanding and accepted my deepest apologies.

On the police radio, a minute later, someone said, "Philbrick, is at East 10th and 25th Street and needs gravy on a '3'. The call sign for a '3' is an emergency. Everyone got a good laugh on my keen vision and astute police work that night. Come on, think about it. Doesn't a large chicken breast and leg look like a gun? Ok, how about at night? Maybe, just a little bit?

Man with a Gun: Learning Point

Sometimes you make a mistake as a police officer, at work or as a parent. If you do, correct the mistake and take responsibility for your actions and then move on. You can't change the past, but you can predict the future. You will know exactly what to do next time.

8.34 Skill or Luck

I was in patrol, working midnights. During roll call that night, the sergeant read a BOLO (Be on the lookout) for a black male that was robbing convenient stores in Hialeah. He was hitting the stores late at night when the cashier was alone. He worked alone and used a 2-inch revolver to rob the stores.

It was early January and pretty cold for South Florida. I was driving to meet another officer for coffee when I drove past the 7-Eleven at West 12th Avenue and 68th Street. It was about 3am. As I drove past the store, I observed a black male standing in front of the store. When he saw me, he picked up the pay phone at the end of the building. That seemed a little suspicious to me. I turned around to check him out.

As I walked up to him, he was leaning against the wall, talking to someone on the phone. He had the telephone receiver in his left hand and his right hand was in his right coat pocket. I always like to see both hands, but it was a cold night.

I walked up to him and said, "What are you doing out in this cold weather?" He turned toward me and said, "It's my boss, talk to him." At the same time, he tried to hand me the phone, I immediately noticed his right hand in his pocket as he extended the phone to me. I looked at the phone and then his face and I knew I was in trouble.

Instinctively, I reached over with my left hand and grabbed his right hand still in his pocket. At the same time, I put my right hand on my Glock pistol in my holster. When I reached out and grabbed his hand in the jacket, I felt a gun. He was holding a 2-inch revolver in the hand hidden in the jacket pocket.

With lightning speed, I drew my gun from my holster and pointed it directly at his face and said, "Slowly take your hand out of your pocket and turn around and face the wall." I had a good grip on his hand on the gun and was squeezing it with all my strength. At the same time, I was pushing the barrel of the gun in his pocket downward toward the ground.

I felt his hand release the gun and I immediately turned him around and put him against the wall. I reached in his jacket pocket and with my left hand, pulled out a loaded Smith & Wesson, 2-inch revolver. I stuck it in my pocket and handcuffed the subject.

I couldn't prove that night that he was the midnight robber, so he went to jail for carrying a concealed firearm.

He had a violent history of arrests including aggravated battery, armed robbery in Georgia, manslaughter and just got out of prison two months previously.

Several days later, a robbery detective called me and told me the subject was responsible for five robberies on the midnight shift. I got a commendation for catching the midnight robber.

Skill or Luck: Tactical Point

Always watch the hands of someone you are tracking. They have aroused your sixth sense for some reason. Listen to your instincts and they will save your life.

Now, was I lucky that I grabbed the hand with the gun in it? No, I think that was a reactive survival skill that I want you to learn. Always watch the person's hands in front of you. If you don't see both hands, you could be in danger. Where I was lucky, was when I grabbed his hand in the jacket, I must have also stopped the revolvers cylinder from moving. That was probably why he couldn't pull the trigger and shoot me through the lining of the jacket pocket. The firearm was pointed at my chest and head.

8.35 The Publix Robbery

I was working plain clothes in May. It was just starting to get hot here in South Florida. I remember that morning because I was on a robbery stakeout at 8am and it was already humid and hot. I was sitting in my unmarked car with the windows down, sweating and trying to stay awake.

Our plain clothes unit had been charting an armed robbery subject who robbed three different victims at two different Publix Supermarkets in our city. His MO, or method of operation, was to rob them in the parking lot as they pulled up to buy groceries. He knew they had money, otherwise, they would not be out shopping.

The robbery subject was described as a black male, mid 30's, 6ft. with a beard and had been seen driving a yellow Volkswagen. He was armed with a large revolver, black in color. In all the robberies, he fled in that yellow Volkswagen.

This morning, we were staking out two different Publix markets. I was with my Lieutenant, and another plain clothes officer on Hialeah Drive. The other robbery suppression team was at a Publix about one mile away. On this stakeout, we were in separate vehicles. I had just pulled up and parked.

We were not there more than twenty minutes, when Lt. Stocker called me on the radio. He got my attention when he said, "Yellow Volkswagen just pulled in." I looked up and, sure enough, there he was. The chances of this guy showing up minutes after we arrived, were nil to none. Nevertheless, there he was.

I told Stocker I had a good visual. The subject was sitting in his car. At this point, it looked like our suspect, but we were not 100% sure. All we had were composite drawings by the victims. I could see him sitting in the Volkswagen, looking around. He had something in his lap that he was holding but I couldn't see what it was. Then he got out.

It was the same robbery subject. I looked at the composite drawing and it was him. This guy was at least 6ft. tall and had a beard. He had targeted an elderly female in a blue Ford. She had just pulled up on the north side of Publix.

After she parked, he approached her. He then pulled the gun from under his front shirt. Her window was down and he put the .38 caliber firearm about two inches from her head. I was not parked that far away. I heard him say, "Give me your purse or I will kill you."

At that point, I was getting out of my unmarked car. I told Stocker on the radio, "Let the robbery go down. Do not stop him from robbing her." He acknowledged, "Roger that." The reason is, you do not want to panic the robber or the victim into doing something stupid. He could shoot her, grab her and take her hostage, shoot me or several other unpleasant variables. The plan was to let him rob her and take him down as he walked away.

After the robbery, she told me the story. The elderly female was confused and when he stated, "Give me your purse," she asked him to repeat it. So, he told her again, but louder, "Give me your fucking purse." What did she do? She put the window up. This forced the armed robbery subject to pull his gun back from inside the car. He just got the gun out in time before the window closed.

He turned around to leave as Stocker and I approached him. As I drew my Glock pistol from my holster, I identified myself and I yelled, "Police officer, put the gun down on the ground." He hesitated for a minute. The gun was still in his right hand. I began to squeeze the trigger on my Glock pistol. I gave him the command one more time. He responded and put both hands in the air while still holding the revolver. I made him put the gun down and told him to lay face down on the pavement. I covered him while Stocker handcuffed the armed robbery subject.

Later, the victim told me, "I don't hear that well and I wasn't sure what he said, so I asked him to repeat it. But, when I saw the gun, I just put the window up." This is one case where an armed robbery was foiled by just rolling up the window.

We arrested the subject and cleared three other armed robberies. He went to jail and was sentenced to twenty years for the four robberies.

The Publix Robbery: Tactical Point

The victim in this robber was lucky. The subject could have been desperate and fired through the window, killing the alleged robbery victim. It was a deterrent that happens a lot in America, but I would recommend giving the robber what they want so you don't get in harm's way.

8.36 Robbery Turned Homicide

It was my first year in homicide, and I had just sat down to dinner. The alert tone announced a robbery in progress at West 7th Avenue and 28th Street. The location was a convenience store. I didn't initially respond because I had just sat down for a nice meal. I could hear officers arriving. Then, the air on the radio was silent for emergency radio transmissions until one of the patrol officers cleared the radio for normal transmissions, as per protocol.

An officer stated, "Dispatch, give me fire rescue to the scene. I've got one down. Also, get me homicide and Criminal ID." I left my dinner after my second bite. Upon arrival, I learned the following:

Two males, both carrying handguns, entered the convenience store and demanded the owners get down on the floor. The robbers told them, "Keep your head down and don't look at us."

The owners were husband and wife. As the robbers removed the cash, cigarettes and other valuable items, the husband, who was face down, was giving one of the robbers an attitude.

After taking the cash, both robbers were exiting the store and the husband on the floor said, "You took everything, assholes, now don't come back."

His wife told me, "After the two robbers had left the store, the shorter of the two men came back inside. He walked over to where we were face down on the floor and stood over my husband and said, "No, you're the asshole." Then he shot my husband twice in the back of his head." Her husband died on the floor of his store.

Robbery Turned Homicide: Learning Point

Don't ever argue, challenge or irritate anyone robbing you with a firearm. Give the subject whatever he wants and hope he goes away and lets you live. Nothing you own is worth dying for.

8.37 Broken ATM

On a Friday night in Hialeah, two ambitious con artists got away with about $10,000 in cash and checks. The two men stood in front of the Barnett Bank and looked very official. Dressed in security guard uniforms and guarding a large, locked metal box, they told all the night deposit customers that the ATM machine was broken and was not accepting deposits. They had jammed the ATM slot with a piece of wood. You couldn't deposit any money in the bank that night.

Numerous customers gladly put their deposit in the large locked metal box. One of the victims stated, "The box even had the name of the bank on the side of it."

Once the con artists got enough deposits, they left. The police did not know anything about the theft until days later. Customers who made their night deposits started calling and asking where their deposit was in their account.

Broken ATM: Banking Protocol

Ask yourself, "Does this look like a normal banking procedure? Two guards and a metal box?" If the ATM is broken, or you suspect anything out of the ordinary, leave that bank and go to another branch. It wouldn't be a bad idea to contact your local police as well. It would only take a few minutes for an officer to arrive and determine if there was a scam or the ATM was actually broken.

8.38 My First Burglar Arrest

It was my first night riding as a police officer. It was midnight patrol. Just after 1:00am, dispatch advised of a burglary in progress. A subject was inside the home- owner's boat on the north side of the house. I was riding with my Field Training Office, Bill Connors.

To be quiet, we parked one house south of the burglary in progress and walked up to the boat. The burglar was still inside the boat on the trailer. As we approached the boat, the burglar lowered a deep-sea fishing rod and reel to the ground.

I looked at Bill and he had his gun out, so I took my gun out also. Bill nodded for me to take over.

I pointed my gun at the burglar in the boat. His back was to me. I said, "Get out of the boat, you're under arrest." When I said that, he jumped. I scared the hell out of him. He turned and I said it again. "Police officer, you are under arrest, get out of the boat." He crawled over the side of the boat and Connors handcuffed him. I was excited because this was my first arrest as a police officer and my first burglar.

I walked him to the police car. I looked at him and expected him to look different. He didn't. I thought he would look demonic or look 'like a burglar' but he was just a 17-year old kid. He looked like every other kid on the block. I was a little disappointed.

My First Burglar: Teaching Point

Don't expect someone who commits a crime to look like a criminal. They look just like you and me.

8.39 Murder on the Phone

One night in Hialeah, around 2:30 am, a hysterical female called the police 911 emergency line and screamed, "He's going to kill me!" The 911 operator said, "Ok, miss, please calm down and tell me what's happening." She said, "My husband is coming over here and he said he was going to kill me when he got here." The operator told the caller, "Mrs. Hernandez, please stay on the phone with me. I have several police officers en-route to your location."

About a minute goes by, while she is talking to dispatch and the caller suddenly starts screaming, "He's here! God help me." Seconds later, dispatch heard and recorded her screaming and four gunshots. The patrol officer's arriving were advised of the situation that shots have been fired and the victim is no longer talking to dispatch.

Uniform patrol units raced to the scene after getting the distress call from the site. The estranged husband came back to his wife's apartment and did, in fact, kill her. When the patrol units arrived, they found the deceased victim on the tile floor near the phone and front door. She had been shot four times. The husband was still in the apartment and was immediately arrested for first degree murder.

Murder on the Phone: Survival Point

This is an example of two errors that permitted the murder of Mrs. Hernandez. First, the victim waited too long to call the police. If she would have called the police when he first threatened her, she might be alive today. Call the police before your life is in danger and not when you are about to be killed.

Secondly, dispatch should have told her to leave the house or barricade herself in the house and find a place to hide. Slow down the shooter and let the police arrive and let them do what they have to do with an armed subject.

Remember one thing. What does it cost you to call the police? The answer is absolutely nothing. You can always cancel the police prior to them arriving.

8.40 Thread of Evidence

When I was a sergeant in homicide, we also investigated sexual battery or rapes. One night, I was working the 4:00 pm to 2:00 am shift. It was about 1:30am and the radio alerted, "Burglary in progress, white male just fled out of the 2nd story apartment."

As luck would have it, the subject who committed the burglary parked in the apartment parking lot. He got into his truck and tried to start his vehicle, but the battery was dead. He was sitting in his truck at 1:32 am at the rear of the apartment complex and his truck wouldn't start. The responding patrol officer quickly placed him into custody.

I arrived and looked at where he entered the apartment. My investigation revealed that he crawled into the apartment through an open window in the living room. It was hot that night and the husband had left the sliding window open for air to circulate into the apartment. The subject pushed the screen in and crawled into the living room. Once inside, he went into the bedroom and took cash out of the tenant's wallet and also stole his wedding band from the dresser.

The man's wife was in bed with him. It was extremely hot and humid that night and the woman had thrown the bed covers off herself. She was lying next to her husband, naked. The burglar, seeing an opportunity, walked over to the side of the bed and sexually fondled the wife. The wife obviously assumed it was her husband touching her. She started to moan. The burglar thought she liked it, so he goes deeper, faster and harder. The wife again, thinking it was her husband, reached up and grabbed the arm that was touching her. It wasn't her husband's arm.

When she opened her eyes and saw a stranger and not her husband, she started screaming. He dropped the stolen jewelry and rapidly exited the front door of the apartment and ran down the stairs to his truck.

As fate would have it, his pickup truck wouldn't start. He had a dead battery. He was arrested for burglary and sexual battery.

I interviewed the emotionally shaken wife. It was dark in her bedroom and the victim stated she would have difficulty identifying the subject. But, as luck or superb investigative skills I discovered a couple of threads from the subject's jeans in the window frame where he had crawled through. He ripped his jeans, crawling into the apartment.

A forensic team positively matched the subject to the apartment using collected threads from the window. The crime lab matched the subject's jeans he was wearing that night to the threads I had collected. The crime scene techs also recovered a partial fingerprint that matched the subject. The burglar's primary goal was to break in and steal jewelry and money. But, when the second opportunity presented itself, he took advantage of it. In this case, the burglar turned rapist.

Thread of Evidence: Forensic Point

Why am I telling you this story? Because I want the reader to realize that in almost every crime, the perpetrator leaves some kind of evidence behind. It could be a shoe print, semen, partial fingerprint or even a small fiber from their clothing. After a crime has occurred, try to preserve the crime scene the best you can.

8.41 Buy a Dog, Buy a Big Dog

I was working patrol as a sector sergeant and I was supervising five uniformed patrol officers. Two of the officers responded to a burglary in progress at a house on West 43rd Street.

Upon arrival, they met the homeowner outside and she said, "I opened the door and saw two men in my living room. I closed the door and called the police. I think they are still in the house."

The officers asked for backup and I started in that direction. After a perimeter was established, the two officers searched the house and did not find the burglars. Both suspects escaped out the back door prior to the police arriving.

The patrol officers brought the homeowner inside to witness her bedrooms and closets completely turned upside-down. The burglars searched every closet, dresser drawer and box, trying to find her valuables. They did get some jewelry and several old silver coins.

I arrived and after about five minutes she asked one of the patrol officers who was taking the report, "Have you seen my dog?" Officer Perez replied, "What dog?" She said, "I have a little poodle named Mimi and I can't find her. If she was here, she would be barking up a storm."

The patrol officers started searching the house and after about ten minutes told the homeowner, "Your dog is not here. It's possible the burglars took your dog."

The homeowner left the room emotionally upset and crying. Meanwhile Criminal ID and the Forensic team had arrived and were dusting the bedroom drawers and jewelry boxes for prints.

I was about to leave when suddenly the homeowner let out a hysterical scream. Everyone rushed to where she was in the kitchen. She found Mimi her little poodle. The burglars had put the barking dog into the freezer. She must have been barking at the burglars, so they opened the freezer door and stuffed the dog inside. The poodle didn't weigh more than six pounds. The dog was dead and partially frozen. I told the victim that if we catch these guys, I will make sure we add the 'cruelty to animals' charge. We never did solve the residential burglary or who killed her little dog.

Buy a Dog, Buy a Big Dog: Lesson from the Case

If you are going to buy a dog that barks, buy a big one that won't fit in your freezer.

8.42 Midnight Audit

I was still a rookie police officer and thought I knew it all. I had been with the police department for about ten months since starting at the academy. Three months of that was in the police academy and the other three months was with a Field Training Officer. I had been riding by myself for about four months.

I was working the midnight shift and was dispatched to a drugstore called, My Pharmacy on an audible burglar alarm. I should have been able to hear the alarm ringing upon arrival, but I didn't hear anything. The only problem was that My Pharmacy had a history of false alarms. False alarms are caused by wind, faulty alarm contacts, insects and large rats.

I was first to arrive and upon exiting my patrol car, I observed a Chevy station wagon backed up to the front doors of the pharmacy. The time was 3:10 am. Still, I was not that suspicious due to the many false alarms at this drug store.

The lights inside the drugstore were on. I tried the front glass door and it opened. I went inside and immediately saw two adult males behind the counter in the pharmaceutical section.

When one of them saw me, he stated, "Midnight audit, no problem, officer." For a brief second, I believed him, but I quickly came to my senses and drew my pistol and yelled, "Put your hands on your head and do it now or I will shoot both of you." They kept saying, "You're making a mistake, we work here." The backup officer arrived after I had both burglary subjects handcuffed and in custody.

Even after cuffing both of the subjects, I still wasn't sure they weren't the owners or auditors. Further investigation revealed that they were former employees who were fired more than three months ago. The two ex-employees were, in fact, burglars. The burglars had wrapped a wet towel around the alarm bell outside. The wet towel muffled the sound of the alarm bell. All you could hear was 'tink, tink, tink' in a very low volume.

Investigation revealed that they still had keys to the store and had filled their car with pharmaceuticals and prescription drugs. Both burglars were sentenced to three years in prison.

8.43 Evidence from a Rape?

Things have changed since I worked homicide many years ago.

At that time, we shared one small refrigerator in the detective bureau. Once in a while, someone would put evidence from a sexual battery or a semen sample in the same refrigerator that we put our cream in that was for or our coffee. The semen sample would only be there for a weekend or a day or two until we shipped it off to the lab for processing.

On this day, Eddie Royal and I played a trick on the rest of the guys in the detective bureau.

In front of several detectives, I asked Detective Royal to clean out all of the old evidence from the refrigerator. Of course, he would find our fake rape evidence. After a few minutes, he found the milk labeled 'semen sample, case number 88-11828.' Just as he was about to throw it away, I said, "Eddie, I would drink that semen for $20. When I said that, half of the guys in the bureau started getting sick. Eddie reached in his pocket and pulled out a $20 bill and threw it on the table. He then said, "Show me, sergeant, there's the twenty."

We now had the riveted attention of about six or seven detectives. He handed me the small cup with the creamy, white liquid in it marked "Evidence." Eddie then said, "This case is closed, there's the twenty." I picked up the cup, opened the clear lid and smelled it. Detectives Bill Porth and Terry Duke were getting sick as I smelled the alleged semen.

I took my time looking at the semen and then I said, "Down the hatch," as I drank the creamy liquid from the clear cup. All of the detectives in the room were disgusted. I heard comments like, "Philbrick, you are one sick dude, man. You are fucked up."

I just replied, "Fastest $20 I ever made."

We didn't tell them it was ice cream, milk and water for a few minutes.

When we finally told everyone, they were relieved, and we all had a good laugh.

8.44 The Case of the Sleeping Burglar

I was a police officer in the uniform patrol division working midnights. One night, around 2am, I was dispatched to a burglary in progress. I arrived with another officer and went to the front door of the house where the call originated. We both had our guns out and started looking for a break-in or the burglar.

The front door opened up and the owner looked at me and the other officer. He put his index finger to his mouth and nose, signaling us to be quiet. "Shhh," he waved us into the house and pointed to the couch. I was confused and really didn't know what to expect.

I walked around the couch and saw a man sleeping. On the table, in front of him, was an open beer can, chips and some ham. Hanging out of his pockets was the owner's jewelry and other valuables. It was like a movie. I couldn't ask for a better place for the stolen jewelry to be.

The owners had been to a party and came home and found the burglar sleeping on their couch. Apparently, he had broken into their house, ate some chips and ham and then drank a beer. He then laid down on the couch and fell asleep. When the homeowners came home from the party, they discovered him in their house on the couch.

According to the state law, the homeowners could have woken him up and shot him. It's called the 'Castle Doctrine' in Florida. Does that make any sense? Not really. They did the right thing by not waking him up and calling the police.

With my partner at the burglar's feet and me standing at his head with our guns out, I gently woke up the sleeping burglar. He opened his eyes, saw us and said, "Damn it." He then put his hands out to be handcuffed.

In the patrol car, I asked the burglar what happened, and he said he had been walking for hours, saw the house with no lights, broke in through the rear door and entered the house. Once inside, he ransacked the bedroom.

Prior to leaving, he looked in the refrigerator and saw the ham and beer. He sat down and drank the beer, ate some ham and chips and fell asleep. As fate would have it, this burglar had an extensive drug problem and committed burglaries to feed his narcotics habit. Maybe a few years in jail might help him kick his drug addiction. Thus ends the case of the sleeping burglar.

The Sleeping Burglar: Law Enforcement Point

Burglary is a serious crime and usually a crime of opportunity. Not many are planned. A lot of burglars carry a weapon when they commit this crime. Those burglars are desperate and will kill if they have to. If you are home and burglars enter your house, call 811 and stay on the phone with dispatch until the police arrive.

8.45 Homicide

After being in the police department for five years, I had a pretty good reputation as a police officer that wasn't afraid to work. I was serious and worked hard at my craft of catching the bad guys. I was Officer of the Month a few times and took the sergeant's exam and finished in the top five applicants.

I was just getting off duty from the afternoon shift and I saw Lieutenant Faulk. He was in charge of Homicide and Robbery. He stopped me in the hallway. Lieutenant Faulk looked at me and said, "I hear you are coming to Homicide." I responded, "I don't think so, lieutenant, I didn't put in for homicide." He looked at me, paused, turned and walked away. As he was walking away, he said, "See you next Monday."

Usually, in law enforcement, if you want to go to a particular specialty unit, you put in a request for transfer and it goes through the chain of command. I didn't put in for homicide. For some reason, I was being transferred from patrol to the detective bureau starting the following Monday.

I made sergeant shortly thereafter and was in charge of the Crimes Against Person's Unit, which included sexual battery, robbery, assaults and homicide.

This was during the time of the Cuban Mariel Boat Lift. The drug dealers were killing each other over cocaine and territorial rights. There were gun fights every day and the gun fights were just beginning.

I didn't speak Spanish very well but could give commands and fill out an arrest affidavit. We received a report of a missing person and went to interview the husband. The report was short and the officer taking the report indicated that there may be foul play involved and the victim missing was extremely suspicious. She was a housewife with two small children. Her sister reported her missing. The missing female, two children and her husband recently arrived from Cuba.

Detective Eddie Royal and I went to the victim's apartment on 17th street. Royal was a very sharp and experienced homicide detective. One of the best.

Through an interpreter, we interviewed the husband who was not very cooperative. His response to the questions were suspicious and didn't make sense. Royal told me to keep him occupied while he snooped around. He walked around the apartment and went outside for a few minutes. While he was outside, one of the neighbors told him, "Look in the trunk of his car."

Detective Royal asked the subject if we could look in his car. He lied and said his wife had the keys to the Buick parked out front. He then said, "If you want to look in my car, go ahead."

He didn't know that we had already seen the keys. When Royal was snooping around, he had seen the keys to the Buick on the bedroom nightstand. The subject signed a consent form for us to search his car, thinking that we didn't have access to the trunk of the vehicle. Royal had the keys.

I searched the interior of the car and found nothing of value. When Royal produced the keys to the car, the subject went wild. I didn't understand exactly what he was saying but he didn't want Royal to search the trunk.

Royal opened the trunk of the car and discovered the body of a twenty-eight year-old female. It was his wife. Eddie Royal, a seasoned homicide detective, looked at the body and told me the victim had been strangled to death. We handcuffed the subject, processed the scene, towed the vehicle and hours later, and tried to interview the subject. He was uncooperative. For over two hours, I tried to interview him and all I got were lies.

One of my seasoned homicide investigators was Jose Gondar. He was from Cuba also and told me he could relate with the subject and possibly gain rapport with him. Maybe he would talk to Detective Gondar. I said, "Sure, go ahead. He wouldn't talk to me. Good Luck."

I left Gondar alone with the subject and started writing the report. After an hour, the detective came into my office and handed me two sheets of paper with writing on them. I asked, "What is this?" Gondor replied, "His confession. He killed his wife because she was cheating on him." He then went through the handwritten confession, highlighting where the subject admits to killing his wife. It was written in Spanish.

I was amazed and quite impressed with Gondar's ability to interview a homicide subject. I then asked him, "How did you get him to confess?"

Standing in my office, he reached over and picked up my telephone book and said, "I hit him with this." I wasn't quite sure what he said, so I asked him again, "What did you do?"

Gondar leaned over and put both arms on my desk and said, "These Mariel refugees are all from Castro's prisons. They know nothing but violence. In Castro's prison, you get beat every day. That is what they understand. I just refreshed his memory."

I got up from behind my desk and walked into the room where Gondar interviewed the subject. He was still handcuffed to the table. He had a few red marks on his face and that was it.

I picked up the phone book and asked Detective Gondar, "This is what you used to get a confession?" He said, "Yes."

We had a confession, but not voluntarily. I really didn't know what to do, so I did nothing. We had a confession.

The subject was sentenced to twenty-five years in prison for killing his wife. I cleared one of my homicides on the board. That year I supervised forty-two homicides, clearing all but seven.

8.46 Wait for the Police

I responded to an audible burglar alarm at a warehouse. I was delayed getting to the warehouse because a train had traveled through the city and it took three to four minutes for the train to clear. By then, the owner of the warehouse, unknown to me, was on the scene.

I parked in the rear and got out. I could hear the alarm bell ringing. It was dark, but a streetlight illuminated part of the warehouse. I looked down between the two buildings and I saw a figure. I immediately drew my 8mm Glock and started yelling, "Police Officer, freeze!" The man turned towards me and I saw a gun in his hand.

I was about fifteen to twenty yards from him and I put my finger on the trigger of my semi-automatic pistol and yelled one more time before I pulled the trigger. I again identified myself and yelled, "Police Officer, drop the gun and get on the ground." I was moving toward him and my backup had just arrived.

The man with the gun yelled back at me, "I'm the owner of the business." I was closer now and I had not shot him because his gun was still pointing down to the ground. I told him one more time, "Put the gun on the ground and put your hands up in the air." He repeated back to me, "I'm the owner." I didn't know who he was and I yelled one more time, "Put the gun on the ground and put your hands up." The man put the gun on the ground and put his hands behind his head. I moved in rapidly and forced him against the wall in an off-balanced position. He had his hands on the wall and his feet were away from the wall. He was completely off balance. I was not sure if this was a burglar or the business owner.

I asked him a few questions. He knew the address of the warehouse and the name of the business. I verified that he was, in fact the owner of the business. I then told him how close I was to shooting him. I told the business owner, "When you call the police, let us do our job. You could have been killed tonight by me or the burglar. By trying to help, you just might have gotten yourself killed." He understood and got the message.

Wait for the Police: Tactical Consideration

Under the cover of darkness, burglars go on the prowl. Cat burglars work high end residential neighborhoods and commercial burglars break into businesses. Most criminals have a set of skills and don't cross over into other crimes they know nothing about. Other thieves steal cars, tires, car batteries, Corvette T tops and more.

For the criminal, it is easy pickings when you have only four officers in a two square mile area. If one of us makes an arrest or gets dispatched to a traffic accident, there goes the other half of zone coverage. The police are spread pretty thin these days.

A lot of professional thieves will have a police scanner and know exactly where each patrol officer is during their shift. They learn the police codes, our locations and how many officers go in service. Criminals will buy police scanners at a store and listen to the calls, counting who is in service, at lunch or clear.

8.47 The Patient Burglar

I was on patrol and dispatched to a residential burglary one morning. When I arrived, I could not believe what the thieves did to gain entry into this house. This burglary took several hours just to get in the house.

During the night, under the cover of darkness, the burglars (multiple), removed an entire set of exterior protective bars from the rear window of the house. After taking off the bars, they removed the entire window frame and windows. They needed a large exit space to take the victim's property out. They knew what they were after.

The set of metal bars that protected the two large bedroom windows took hours to remove from the house. The security bars were bolted to the exterior of the house and then tap coned into the wall.

They must have been friends of the victim because the removal of the windows and bars took special tools. They were not your usual metric design but totally different. Someone had knowledge of this home's windows.

As in many cases, the burglars knew that the house contained valuable items. The burglars definitely knew the victim. The owner was a jeweler and was in the hospital for diabetes issues. The thieves financially wiped him out of everything he had at home and more. His personal losses totaled over $60,000. The thieves knew he had large pieces of artwork and that is why they removed the bars and windows. Many times, when you are the victim of a burglary, you know the thieves.

The Patient Burglar: Crime Prevention Tip

My point here is that even though you have fortified your home, it is still vulnerable. Remember the Secret Service rule, concentric circles of security. The more layers of security you have, the less chance of your security being penetrated. An inside motion alarm or a window alarm would have prevented this loss.

8.48 Road Rage Shooting

In 2003, I handled a case in which the driver of a vehicle was shot at from another car. The victim of the shooting told me he accidentally cut off the other vehicle. When the driver blew his horn after being cut off, the victim gave the driver the finger. That is when he saw the gun.

After giving the guy the finger, he saw the rear passenger from the other car lean out of the window. He was holding a small semi-automatic pistol. The driver slowed down and the subject in the rear seat started shooting. The victim told me that he fired at least two, maybe three shots at him. To stop them from shooting anymore, he turned off the expressway. After hearing the gun shots, he felt the impact under his seat. The subject then changed lanes and fled.

One of the 8mm bullets penetrated the door and ricocheted off the base of the seat and then up through the cushion. The bullet was recovered after slightly bruising the victim. The bullet had no velocity and did not break the skin of the driver. In fact, it actually hit his wallet and stopped there. He pulled over and called 811.

The driver was lucky. We never did solve the shooting.

Road Rage Shooting: Tactical Consideration

It is not worth it! If you are involved in a road rage with anyone, you must drive away. It doesn't matter what they say or do, just turn off at the next turn and live to tell the story. You have no idea who the road rage subject is. I have seen people killed over parking spots, domino games and road rage. Be smart. Just drive away!

8.49 Auto Thieves, the Key Maker

On this particular day, I was in plain clothes at the Westland Mall. We would park in the parking lot and just sit there. You would be amazed at what you see and what takes place in a shopping mall when you just sit somewhere and observe.

I had been watching a vehicle for about ten minutes that was acting suspicious in the parking lot. At one point, the blue Ford occupied by two males pulled up next to a Cadillac. The passenger leaned over and appeared to have tried the driver's door. A minute later, the car pulled away and went eastbound. I radioed another team member named Sandy and told him the car was headed his way.

He said, "I got it. It's parked over here near the Sears entrance." The vehicle traveled back to the west side of the mall and again pulled up next to the Cadillac.

I was about a hundred yards away. I was looking through binoculars but I could still see that the subject in the passenger seat was leaning over and doing something with the driver's door of the Cadillac. I radioed this to another team member and got more units in the area.

The Ford pulled away from the Cadillac and parked near Sears again. I was a little confused as to what they were doing. I decided to take them down if they went back to the Cadillac or left the mall.

The Ford travelled back to the Cadillac and this time, the passenger got out and walked over to the Cadillac, put a key in the driver's door, opened it and got in. I told all of the unmarked units to take both subjects down.

At the same time, all of the tactical officers arrived, and at gunpoint, took down the Ford and ordered the subject out of the Cadillac. I was not sure what we had, but I believed they were trying to steal the Cadillac.

Investigation revealed that they were making a key for the Cadillac in their Ford. They had a key grinder in the glove compartment box, fully operational, powered and hundreds of blank keys. This was remarkable. They could make any vehicle key from inside their vehicle.

What the passenger was doing was putting the 'soft' blank key in the Cadillac keyhole, moving it around and marking it by the movement. He would then drive away, cut the key and go back and try it again on the door. After about three times, he had cut a perfect key that would open the Cadillac door and start the ignition.

Not only were these two auto thieves stealing cars, but they were giving the new owner a set of perfect keys.

Auto Thieves the Key Makers: Tip

If the cars they attempted to steal had a car alarm, they would have moved on to another vehicle, not yours. Lock your vehicle all the time and keep valuables out of sight. If burglars look into your car and see nothing, they will break into another car where they can see a briefcase, purse or a computer.

8.50 Traffic Accident?

I was at the Westland Mall, positioned on the roof of Burdines surveilling the parking lot for purse snatchers, auto burglaries, auto theft or any other crime.

Just north of Sears, I observed a parked vehicle. The white female driver exited the car and just stood by the driver's door, looking around. At this time, I noticed that she had some damage to her right front quarter panel. The headlight, right quarter panel and hood were all damaged and the car was missing a bumper.

After three or four minutes, she went to the rear of her vehicle and opened the trunk. By herself, she dragged the missing front bumper that belonged to her car and placed it in front of her car. The bumper was severely damaged. She then went back to her trunk and removed a plastic bag and walked to the front of her car where the vehicle damage was and emptied the bag onto the parking lot. The bag was partially filled with dirt and the broken red glass from her broken turn signal. She then kicked the broken glass and dirt around a little bit. She made it look like someone hit her car in the mall parking lot. After that, she was observed next to her car on the phone.

After five minutes, one of our patrol units pulled up and was talking to the female that was apparently involved in an accident. I knew the patrol officer and after a few minutes, asked him to QSY (change channels on his radio.) "Hey Prentice, its Philbrick here, what do you have there?" Officer Prentice said, "No big deal. It's just a hit and run. She said she parked here, went inside and came out and someone had hit her car and fled."

I came down off the roof and went to where Officer Prentice was. I told him what I had observed, and he arrested the Latin female for filing a false police report and another charge with regards to the accident.

She thought she could unload all the pieces from her prior accident and then call the police and report a hit and run.

She went to jail for a short period of time.

8.51 Sexual Predator

In our plain clothes unit, we worked Westland Mall at least three or four days out of the week. The predators and thieves knew everyone going in the mall had money and would most likely be away from their parked cars for a least thirty to forty-five minutes. It was easy pickings for a seasoned criminal.

On this particular day, Officer Sandy Flutie was on the roof. I was in an unmarked police car. I was the chase unit. My job was to stop any offenders before they left the mall.

From the Burdines roof, you could see about half of the shopping mall. Flutie had seen a Mustang make several passes around the mall but could not get a good visual on the car or the driver. I quickly drove to that area of the mall and got behind the car Sandy had identified as being suspicious. I followed the car but quickly turned off to give the driver space. I told Sandy that the red Mustang was coming his way.

He was tracking the Mustang. About the third time the vehicle drove by his area, he radioed, "I've got a good visual on the Mustang. It is a white male driving and he ….he's…..naked! I repeat, the subject has no clothes on."

The male in the Mustang was driving around the shopping mall completely naked in his car. I stopped the vehicle. I cautiously approached the driver and told him to slowly exit the vehicle. He looked back at me and said, "I can't get out."

I told him to put some pants on. He exited the car, wearing a pair of nylon shorts and nothing else. I asked him why he was driving around naked. His response was, "There's no law against it."

I ran his criminal background and learned that he was a registered sex offender. I arrested him for indecent exposure, loitering and prowling.

About a month later, the case went to court. The defense attorney requested a trial by the judge and not a jury. I agreed due to what Flutie and witnessed after stopping he naked driver. I thought the case was pretty cut and dry.

After an hour of court procedures the judge ruled on the case. I lost the case and all charges were dropped. The judge stated the reason was,

"Due to only Officer Flutie seeing the naked subject in the vehicle and not the general public he dismissed all charges.

His attorney argued that his client's vehicle had the same expectations of privacy as his home. Also from Flutie's vertical position on the roof, he was able to see in the car, whereas, the general public could not.

The judge agreed and dropped the charges. Can you believe that?

8.52 Miami Dolphins

If you are a police officer and an employed by your municipality, it is your duty to provide a professional service to your community. That service may take the form of helping stranded motorists, transporting elderly females, buying the homeless a meal or helping out where you can.

In zone one in Hialeah, there were some homeless people, but not that many. When I patrolled this sector, I got to know one particular homeless man who lived behind a convenient store on Okeechobee Road. He would eat the food they threw out in the trash. It sounds worse than it really was. The discarded food was donuts, meat pies and sandwiches. The sandwiches were one or two days old and still in the wrapper. The store had a policy to always sell fresh food. This homeless man, Julio would go to the dumpster late at night and feast on the food they threw out.

He got beat up one night and that was our first meeting. Another homeless male assaulted him and took his radio. I'm not sure it even worked. That night, he was the victim of a strong-armed robbery. The thief punched him a few times and took the radio. I had fire rescue check him and he was fine. Julio had no criminal history at all. He was not very sociable. When you spoke to Julio, you knew he wasn't the sharpest tool in the shed. I don't think he was dumb, but he had some mental problems.

One day, I saw him behind the convenient store, and it had just rained. He was soaked, shivering and extremely dirty. His long pants had grease stains, his shirt was black with dirt and his socks looked like he hadn't changed them in months. I knew I had to do something to help him out.

That night, after getting off duty, I went home and prepared a package for him that I would take to him the next day.

The next morning, I found him where he usually stays. I gave him a bottle of Brut men's cologne, body wash, soap, shampoo and clothes. I also gave him a twenty-eight-dollar official NFL Miami Dolphins shirt that I got for Christmas. It was too small for me.

My partner that day was Fred Elfman. We made Julio take a bath from the garden hose at the rear of the restaurant where he sleeps at night. I made him use the shampoo and cologne I gave him. He looked great in his sweatpants and Dolphin shirt. I also gave him a kit with a toothbrush, deodorant, and hairbrush in it. I really felt good about getting Julio clean, dry and in new clothes.

Julio was looking good. He was showered and clean, and now, a Dolphin fan. That day, helping Julio, made Fred and I feel we were giving back to our community.

I then asked him to bag up his old clothes. I didn't want to touch them in case he had lice which was very common in the homeless population. He put his dirty shirt, pants, underwear and socks in a plastic bag that I used to bring the stuff in. I walked over to a nearby dumpster and threw the bag in. I then gave him ten dollars cash and said, "You look good, man. Go get some lunch." He didn't say much. I know one thing; he did not thank me and Fred for our good deed. Fred and I didn't need kudos, we just felt good about what we did that day.

Two days later, I was driving down Okeechobee Boulevard, and I see Julio. Much to my surprise, he was not wearing the orange Miami Dolphin shirt and clothes. He was wearing his old dirty, greasy pants, filthy socks and black stained shirt that I threw in the dumpster. He was back in the same clothes we threw away.

After we left, he must have taken off his new clothes and put back on his dirty ones. I guess he felt more comfortable in them than the clothes I gave him. Oh well, at least we tried.

Miami Dolphins: Lesson learned

Sometimes, people don't want help. They are happy, content and satisfied in their own environment. It might be better just to let them exist in their world without our interference.

8.53 Sedano's Meats

I was bored one day and decided to surveil a parking lot where a string of car burglaries had been occurring. I was in plain clothes, working in the SWAT-Tac Unit. This was a plain clothes unit that did just about everything, such as surveillance, vice and narcotics. We could buy or sell narcotics under a kilo. Just the small stuff. The narcotics unit handled the large quantity sales.

I was sitting in my car and I observed a Latin male exit Sedano's grocery store. He came out and got in his vehicle. After a minute or two, he went back inside the store. On his third trip out of the store, I took the time to observe him.

He got into the driver's seat of a bronze Chevrolet. Once inside the car, I saw him leaning over either picking something up or putting something on the front seat or floor. After a few minutes, he got out of the car and went back into the store. I got out of my car and walked over to his vehicle and looked in the passenger window.

On the floor of his car was packaged meat from the store. There were no bags. I could see packages of steaks, sausages and chicken. I counted at least twelve packages of meat. The guy was stealing meat.

I went back to my car, called for backup and waited. After about ten minutes, he came out again. I noticed he was walking a little stiff and was wearing his shirt out to hide the meat stuffed in his belt line.

He got to his vehicle and I approached him and identified myself. I asked him to put his hands on his car and I pulled his shirt up and there were five packages of steaks and ribs. I put them on his hood and got the other meats from his front seat. In all, he had sixteen packages of meats valued at over $250. I asked the store manager to come outside.

Before the manager came outside, I wanted to run the subject to see if he had any active warrants and a valid driver's license. He had no identification at all. He did not have a driver's license and the car came back to his girlfriend. I really couldn't find out who he was unless I arrested him.

I was feeling pretty good. I was going to arrest this guy and recover a lot of meat that belonged to Sedano's. The manager came out and I showed him all the meat he stole. After a few minutes, the manager told me he didn't want to press charges.

I explained to the Sedano's manager that he had no identification and no driver's license and I didn't know who he was. He didn't care. He just wanted his meat back.

I gave the meat back to the manager and on the side, I explained to him that these guys are professional shoplifters. He thanked me for recovering the meat and said, "Have a nice day." I told the subject/thief, he could leave.

The subject got in the Chevy and drove across the parking lot. After about fifty feet, I pulled in behind him and stopped him. I have a small blue light for emergencies or traffic stops.

I approached his car and asked him to exit the vehicle. Once he got outside of the car, I asked him for his driver's license. He looked at me and said, "You know I don't have one."

That's when I said, "That's right and you're under arrest."

Sedano's Meats: Moral of the Story

This guy needed to go to jail for something. I accommodated him.

8.54 DUI

I was northbound on Red Road just after 2:00 am, when I spotted a Cadillac in front of me driving erratically and swerving from lane to lane. I watched him for a minute and decided to stop him. He was a danger to anyone on the road. I got behind him and put on my blues. The driver immediately pulled over. For safety reasons, as a police officer, I usually tell the driver to come back to me.

From my driver's door in a very authoritative voice, I said, "Driver, exit the vehicle and walk back to the sound of my voice." His window was down, and he opened the car door. He somehow got out of the vehicle without falling over. He then walked back to me, using his vehicle to support him. This guy could hardly stand up; let alone drive.

He got back to my vehicle and I asked him for his driver's license, insurance card and vehicle registration. He took his wallet out and dropped it. With caution, I reached down and picked it up and handed it to him. When I gave him his wallet back, I got a little closer to him and could smell alcohol on his clothing and his breath. At that moment, he started to fall. I caught him and asked him, "Sir, have you been drinking tonight?" He replied, "I've had a couple."

I looked at his driver's license and he was a Hialeah resident. I then asked him, "Mr. Davis, how many drinks have you had tonight?" He looked at me and was nodding his head up and down ever so slightly, but didn't say anything.

I was getting a little upset and I said, "Sir, I'm not going to ask you again. How many drinks have you had tonight?" He looked at me as he swayed from left to right and put his index finger in the air and said, "Give me a minute, I'm still counting."

I just started laughing. I respected his honesty, put him in a cab and sent him home.

DUI: Training Outline

Sometimes having a good laugh is more important than putting someone in jail.

8.55 Send It Back, No Thanks

In Miami-Dade County, there was a chain of restaurants called Ranch House. It was good food, open 24/7, and they gave a 50% discount to the police. The discount was nice but most of the police officers just added more to the waitresses' tip to compensate for not paying full price. I enjoyed eating there. The food was good and the coffee was excellent.

Officer James Swann and I had just handled a traffic accident and we decided to meet at the Ranch House on West 84th Street for lunch. I arrived first and secured a table in the rear of the restaurant. You don't want to sit in the front for safety purposes. There are cases where shooters have walked into a restaurant and killed police officers who were sitting down having lunch. That is why we always sit in the back of a restaurant with our backs to a wall.

Jimmy ordered the lunch burger, well done, and I ordered breakfast. The food came quickly, and we started to eat. Jimmy took one bite out of his burger and noticed it was rare, very rare. He flagged down the waitress and sent it back to the cook.

After four or five minutes, his burger arrived with new French fries. Swann started to eat his burger. It was perfect, except for one thing.

After taking two or three bites, I looked down at Swann's burger and noticed something that shouldn't be there. I wasn't sure what it was, but I knew it didn't belong in between the pickle and onions. I took my fork and lifted up one of the pickles. There was a good one-inch, dead cockroach looking out between the buns. I quickly pointed it out to Jimmy, and he called the waitress over.

She apologized and said, "I don't know how that bug got into your sandwich." She then looked around, leaned over and whispered to Jimmy and me, "I didn't tell you this but all of our cooks are on a work release program from the Dade County jail."

Send It Back, No Thanks: Lesson Learned

That is why you never send food back when you are eating on duty in uniform. The cook has no idea who the food was being delivered to unless you send it back. The restaurant hired cheap labor from the local jails.

These cooks had been arrested for rape, aggravated battery, grand theft, robbery and more. Now they were cooking my lunch.

So, if a waitress asks me, "How is your food?" My answer is always, "Perfect." I don't send anything back anymore.

8.56 Riot Food

In May, 1980 the city of Miami was besieged by riots. More than 300 people were injured and 18 people were killed. Stores were burned and looted after a black male, Arthur McDuffie was killed by the Miami Police. Hialeah defended the cities borders by blocking off the entrances to the city. Every vehicle was stopped, questioned and searched.

I was assigned to the intersection of NW 37 Avenue and 62 Street. We had about eight police officers there and the National Guard. I had my marked unit in the intersection with my blue lights on. Blocks away you could hear the gun shots and the victim's vehicle accelerate as they tried to escape the gauntlet and get to the police.

At our post, we had more than ten civilian vehicles shot up with bullet holes arrive at our intersection. Many of the occupants didn't know there was a riot and drove through the area. Men, women and children were wounded from the gun fire and were taken to the hospital.

Many of the restaurants were closed. Most cities just shut down and everyone stayed at home. The police department was on the Alpha Bravo shift. Everyone was working twelve-hour shifts or more. Most of the officers brought food and coffee from home during the first two or three days of the riots. After that, food and coffee was scarce.

Miami-Dade County, in their infinite wisdom, decided to feed the police with the same food they fed the inmates. It's nothing fancy. For lunch, the inmates got a ham and cheese sandwich, chips and an apple or a banana.

The rioting, burning and looting mostly occurred at night but some areas of Dade County and Hialeah were targets so we just pulled up in front of a store or mall, parked our marked unit out front and went to sleep. One officer stayed awake while the other officers slept. Some of us never went home for three or four days. We slept at the station or in front of someone's business. We ate when we could find food, or our families brought it to us.

After the third day, we started getting boxes of food from the Miami-Dade County Police. In the box, were sandwiches wrapped in paper and a bag of chips or an apple. It was ham or turkey. You got what was handed to you. The sandwiches were not fancy. Some had mustard, some had mayo and some had nothing.

When the food arrived on the fourth day, I thanked the correctional officer for delivering the food and I just happened to say to him, "Thanks for making the sandwiches and fruit plates." He replied, "I didn't make them, the inmates did."

I clarified his response and asked, "You're telling me that the prisoners and inmates made the sandwiches that the police officers working the riots are eating?"

He replied, "Yes sir." I then asked him, "Do your other correctional officers eat this food?" He replied, "Hell no! The inmates made these sandwiches and they were told they were for the police officers out in the field."

From that day on, nobody ate the food delivered to us from the prison or county jail. Some of us ate the fruit or anything canned. Most of the food went to waste.

Miami Dade County, "thanks for the good food."

8.57 Cuban Divorce

You see a lot of terrible things as a police officer. For me, it was always seeing injured or dead children. They are the real victims because they trust their parents to do the right thing and keep them safe. Here is one story where that didn't happen.

It was a quiet Sunday morning and I was about ten minutes from calling it a day. Patrol officers usually get back to the station about twenty-five minutes before their shift is over. They gas up the car, turn in their reports, etc.

I was headed toward the station when the alert tone went off. There was a long high-pitched tone and then dispatch stated, "3-30 (shots fired) at 634 W. 43rd Street. Advise on fire rescue upon arrival."

I wasn't that far away and arrived with Officer Kerrigan, an officer in my zone. The house was in a residential area. We drew our guns and approached the front door. It was quiet from inside the house. I had my ear against the door. I didn't hear anything.

One of the neighbors signaled me to come over and talk to her. As I approached her, she told me, "Five shots. I heard five shots." I thanked her and joined the other officer at the front door. Officer Kerrigan said to me, "How do you want to handle this?" I replied, "Let's go in hard and fast." Dennis and I were both on the SWAT Team.

I kicked the door in and both of us entered the single story house. We were moving fast as we searched. Nothing in the garage or kitchen. When we got to the living room, I could not believe what I saw. It was as clear today as it was over twenty years ago.

Lying on the couch, was a middle-aged Latin female, wearing a blue flowered dress. She may have been thirty-one or thirty-two years old. She had two gunshot wounds. One was in her chest and another to her temple. She wasn't moving.

I looked down on the beige carpet that was covered with blood and saw a little boy. He wasn't more than five or six. He was prone, facing down. I rolled him over to check for vitals. He was shot twice. He was dead also.

Sitting in a Lazy Boy chair was the father. He was holding a .357 six-inch revolver in his right hand. The gun was bloody but still in his open hand. He was alive. He had just killed his entire family and shot himself in the chest.

The husband was still alive and gasping for air. His chest would rise and fall as he tried to take a deep breath. He was wheezing with each attempt to breathe.

Officer Kerrigan raised his radio to call fire rescue. I reached over and slowly pushed the radio down and said, "Fuck this guy. Let him die." He did, about two minutes later.

This was very common in Hialeah. The father kills the entire family rather than get a divorce and lose his kids. Seeing children shot and killed haunts me to this day. I handled three 'Cuban divorces' during my police career.

8.58 Burglary of a Police Vehicle

When I worked plain clothes, we would chart crime statistics and patterns and set up in that area to prevent any further crimes. Criminals, like good fishermen, will work an area or a lake until it is 'fished out.'

Our unit, SWAT-Tac, would try to predict where the next crime would occur based on patterns of movement. In the eastside warehouses, the burglars were hitting any and all vehicles parked overnight in the district.

On this particular night, I was the decoy. I was in a fairly new van with TV logos on the panels of the truck. It looked like a truck that delivered new televisions. I parked at East 10th Avenue and 23rd Street and waited. The takedown team was hiding about three or four blocks away. Everyone was in place and waiting for the bad guys to see the truck and hopefully break into it.

At around 2:15 am, I observed a vehicle drive by twice. That is out of the ordinary at this time of the morning. I tried raising Sgt. Miller to let him know I had company. He didn't answer. After a few minutes, I heard a car pull up behind the van I was hiding in and turn their engine off. I raised Miller on the radio again and he didn't answer. Sgt. Miller and the takedown team were two blocks away and apparently couldn't see the van I was in.

I heard two Latin males say something in Spanish and then someone tried to open the driver's door. I was laying down in the back of the van with my gun in my right hand and my radio in my left. I tried raising Miller again, I whispered, "Are you seeing what they are doing? I think they are trying to get in the van."

Then someone tried to open the passenger door. He shook the door and tried to open the sliding door on the side of the van. Then I saw one of them with a slim jim, trying to open the passenger door.

Shit, I was freaking out. Were these guys armed? Was I by myself? Where was Miller and the take-down team?

I raised Miller again. Finally, he answered, "Go ahead." I whispered and tried to be as quiet as I could, "Two males are trying to break into the van. I repeat, two males breaking into the van."

Obviously, Miller had no idea what was going on and yelled on the radio, "Speak up, I can't hear you." Now, I'm pissed, and I yelled into the radio, "Two burglars breaking into the van, come now!"

The two burglars had the passenger door open but heard me and ran back to their vehicle. Miller and his team used their vehicles to block in the two burglars and take them down at gun point.

They all got a good laugh out of the night, but I didn't think it was so funny.

8.59 Undercover Cop

On this night I was working in a crack neighborhood. Everyone in the neighborhood was profiting from selling crack cocaine on the street corners. On an average day the dealers would gross $12,000 to $15,000 dollars in crack sales. Everyone was making money.

We were looking for a "CI" or a confidential informant, someone that could infiltrate the drug dealers. We tried a few undercover cops but the crack dealers wouldn't bite. We needed an inside informant to eventually make the arrests and hopefully shut it down.

One night I was speaking with one of the local drug kingpins and he asked me if I needed money. He knew who I was even though I was in plain clothes. I said, "Sure, who doesn't need extra cash? My police check gets smaller every week." I figured he wanted to bribe me. He then said, "Maybe we can work something out to help you." I didn't respond back to what he said.

He was part of an organized crack ring that was doing over eighty grand a week, selling crack in the neighborhood and other areas. The drug dealers hired ten and eleven-year old kids to alert the dealers if the police arrived. They had security two and three streets away. Most everyone in the neighborhood was part of the drug group.

That night, I talked it over with my lieutenant and we agreed to test the bad guys to see if they would bite. He told me, "If they approach me again and offer me money, to take it."

That night, the main drug dealer took me the side and offered me cash for information. All I had to do was call them when our unit was about to raid their street vendors. I asked him, "How much money are we talking about." He replied, "It's more than you make in a week." I told him, "Sure, I'm in."

The only people who knew I was going undercover and taking a bribe was one sergeant, one lieutenant, our captain and the police chief. They all agreed if I could infiltrate the drug ring, to do it.

Prior to going undercover, I asked the police chief, captain and lieutenant to sign an affidavit stating that I was not a corrupt cop but was going undercover and could accept bribes, cash, etc. They all signed.

Shortly thereafter, I went undercover as a disgruntled cop in a crack cocaine neighborhood. As part of my assignment, I wore a wire that was monitored by the Florida Department of Law Enforcement (FDLE). Every day before I went to Seminola, the drug sales area, I had to get wired. Sometimes I wore the wire and other times FDLE would put it in my car. I lived the life of a corrupt and dirty cop for more than three months.

I now was an undercover cop taking bribes. It was never the amount they originally offered me but bottom line, they were bribing a law enforcement officer. I would tell the drug dealers when SWAT was coming and where we were going to hit. I also staged arguments with other police officers in front of the drug dealers. All of my friends, fellow police officers and the drug dealers thought I had gone corrupt by taking the cash bribe.

Some things I would do was tell the drug dealers our days off, who was working, and what shifts. This was always cleared by my chain of command who knew I was undercover.

Sometimes when a patrol officer was in the area I would drive by and see what he or she was doing. Many times I was told to mind my own business and let patrol do what they have to do. It was a difficult time for me. I couldn't tell anyone I was working undercover.

Some of my friends, who did not know I was undercover, took me to the side and said, "What the fuck Philbrick?

It was a very tough three months for me, personally. I would protect the drug dealers and talk shit about the police department and how bad the police treated the brothers in Seminola. All my police buddies and friends quit talking to me and inviting me to eat with them. I was having coffee alone a lot. I was undercover and in deep with the dealers and couldn't tell anyone.

During that time, I learned how much money they were making, where they were buying the crack, who was selling it to them, and the identity of all the drug dealers in the organization. After a shift I would meet with FDLE and write a report on the day's information.

They were making a fortune. Each weekend, they would sell on the three different street corners and would gross more than $25,000 to $30,000 in crack sales. In a week, they would sell over $80,000. They were running a multi-million-dollar narcotics business from a street corner. Even the local juveniles were on the payroll as lookouts. Everyone had new cars, new houses, diamonds, jewelry and all the cash they could spend. Until the sting ended.

One night I drove into Seminola and one of the dealers approached my car. He was leaning into the passenger side window and started looking all over the interior of my car. He was looking for a microphone. As usual, I would say their name for the wire. When I said, "What's up Big Daddy, he said, "Nothing Philbrooks, he then turned and walked away." That is when I knew, they knew I was wired. Later we found out one of the narcotics detectives from our police department was banging one of the whores in Seminola and told her.

The next day, three of the major drug dealers invited me to go out on their boat that weekend. I declined telling them I was going to a Miami Dolphin game. So now, all of my friends think I'm dirty and the bad guys want to take me deep sea fishing. I recommended to the Chief of police to end my undercover assignment.

After three months, we had learned enough information to serve warrants on all the players in the drug network. All the dealers were on tape, talking to me. After numerous meetings with FDLE, ATF, and the State Attorney's office we had the probable cause to make the arrests in Seminola

One month later around 4:00 am, the Hialeah Police SWAT Team, FDLE, FBI, ATF, US Customs and about sixty police officers and agents served narcotics search warrants on all the drug dealers. We hit nine houses and two stores at the exact same time. More than thirty-five people went to jail.

When we hit the houses at 4:00 am, I made entry on one of the top narcotic traffickers. Most of the dealers and suppliers all carried guns. To make our entry safer and faster one of the team members shattered the drug dealer's rear sliding glass door. We were in the house within seconds.

I quickly moved down the hallway checking rooms as I cleared the house. I found my subject still in bed. On his night stand was a Glock handgun and a lot of cash rolled up with a rubber band around it. The SWAT Team made entry so fast he didn't have time to wake up and go for his firearm.

While I was handcuffing him, he looked at me suspiciously and said, "Philbrooks, I thought you were with us." (The dealers all called me Philbrooks.) I just said, "You know, you just don't know who you can trust these days" as I handcuffed him and escorted him outside.

8.60 The Phantom Chase

When it was slow on midnights, we would chase each other around the warehouses in our police vehicles. It was good training to keep our driving skills sharp. Right?

I was chasing Wayne Bars and I lost him in the warehouses. I really just got bored, but he kept driving fast. He thought I was still chasing him. He was driving a brand new, marked police unit. During our practice chases, we got up to speeds of 60 to 70 miles per hour.

I stopped chasing him and pulled over and to finish writing a police report for a stolen car. It was about 1:00 am. About a minute later, Officer Bars got on the radio and asked me to QSY (change radio channels). It's a frequency where you can talk freely with another officer. He asked me where I was.

Philbrick, "What's up, Wayne? I'm at East 10 and 11 Street."

Bars, "Can you come over to southeast 11th Avenue and 14th Street? I want to show you something."

I acknowledged that I was en-route and drove to his location. When I arrived, I couldn't believe what I saw. Wayne's brand new, marked police vehicle was virtually wrapped around a cement light pole. The windshield was busted and the front bumper was almost touching the rear bumper. Wayne told me later, he had to crawl out the window to get out of the wrecked car.

The first thing I said was, "Are you injured?"

Wayne responded, "No, but I wrecked the car."

I asked, "What happened?"

Bars, "I thought you were still chasing me, and I lost control. This cement light pole jumped out in front of me and I ran into it."

Philbrick, I didn't find any humor in what he just said. I asked him, "You want me to call the sergeant?"

Bars, "No, I don't want a day off for the accident. Give me a minute while I think about what I'm going to do."

After a minute or so, Wayne said to me, "Watch this."

He crawled back into his vehicle through the window, started the car, engine was still operational, and turned on his siren and emergency equipment. He was sitting in his car that was wrapped around a cement pole and got on the radio and said, "2315 Chase." He was on the radio telling dispatch that he was now in a chase with another vehicle.

Dispatch, "2315 QSK (go ahead)"

He was now stationary in a police car that was wrapped around a light pole. He was revving his engine, lights and siren screaming and telling dispatch that he was in a high-speed chase.

I didn't want any part of this, so I got in my car and drove away.

As I drove away, I heard on the radio "2315, it's a black Mustang, westbound on SE 16th Street from 12th Avenue.

Dispatch repeated, "2315 in pursuit of a black Mustang westbound on SE 14th Street from 12th Avenue."

Seconds later, Bars stated, "2315 north on SE 11th Avenue approaching 14th Street. Dispatch repeated it again.

There was silence for a few seconds and then, on the radio, Officer Bars stated, "2315, I've lost the Mustang. I'm involved in an accident at SE 11th and 14th Streets. Send fire rescue and a supervisor."

I returned to the scene as if I had never been there and arrived about the same time as fire rescue. They removed Officer Bars from the wrecked vehicle and took him to the hospital. He was complaining about neck and back pain.

Wayne Bars was not disciplined for the accident due to his statement that he was in pursuit of a suspicious black Mustang.

We never did locate the black Mustang. Gee, I wonder why?

8.61 Rapist Arrested

It was just after 2:00 am and I was working the midnight shift. I was riding with my FTO, Bill Connors. I had been out of the academy about six weeks when an alert tone from dispatch sounded on the radio, indicating that a crime was in progress. When the tone was announced, all patrol officers and detectives stood by to receive the address and nature of the emergency call. No one was permitted to speak unless they had an emergency greater than the call being dispatched.

Dispatch advised a rape had just occurred and the subject ran out of the residence. He was described as a white male, in his 30's, wearing a white pullover shirt and jeans. The dispatcher gave the address and my FTO and I were about five blocks away. I was driving and tuned my marked unit around and advised dispatch that we were in the area. I was no more than a block away, when I spotted a white male, no shirt, and jeans walking rapidly away from the area of the dispatched call. I knew this was our subject due to the fact he was carrying one of his boots in his hand and only had one boot on. I guess he left somewhere in a hurry. Connors told me to block his path with the patrol car. I turned into the subject and using my patrol car, blocked him in between another vehicle and a hedge.

I heard her tell the detective that she did not set her house alarm because her boyfriend was due home that night. As bad luck would have it, a rapist broke into her house and attacked her. He did not harm her children.

The subject, using two screwdrivers, lifted the sliding glass door off its track, making entry into the house. If she would have set her perimeter alarm for her residence, she would not have been the victim of a sexual battery.

Rapist Arrested: Tactical Point

You must secure your house to prevent being a victim. Crimes like this occur every day in America. Get the best alarms, good door locks and maybe a big dog that barks. It's not the size of the dog but the sound of the bark keeps burglars away.

8.62 Officer Manny Pardo

Manuel "Manny" Pardo was a police officer in Sweetwater, Florida. He was a patrol officer and even made sergeant at his police department. It took him a few years to learn he could make more money as a dishonest cop then a police officer paid an hourly salary.

I knew Manny Pardo. Manny and I went to college together. We were both in the Master's Program at Barry College. He had been a police officer for three years when he started ripping off drug dealers, using his police badge and uniform. After he ripped them off for drugs and cash, he would kill them.

He was suspected of killing at least nine drug dealers. On his last robbery, he got shot in the leg by one of the dealers. He couldn't go to a local hospital in South Florida but he needed medical treatment.

Hospital protocol states that any gunshot wound must be reported to the local police. Manny couldn't go to Jackson Hospital with his gunshot wound. So, Manny, with a bullet wound in his leg, wrapped his bloody leg and flew to New York. After a day in New York, he filed a police report in Long Island that someone tried to rob him. He told the New York police that he resisted and a Latin male shot him after taking his money. Now he could go to the hospital with the bullet hole in his leg.

The ER doctor's in New York noticed something suspicious about the gunshot. The wound was not fresh. He had been shot three days before in Miami. They question him about the time line and he-Manny made the mistake of telling the New York Police he was a cop in Miami.

After the NYPD notified the Miami-Dade County Police, two detectives flew to New York and recovered the bullet they took out of his leg. Miami-Dade County Police suspected Manny Pardo in several homicides but needed more proof to arrest him.

Ballistics ran the projectile through NCIC and found that the bullet belonged to one of the guns recovered at a drug related homicide. They found a dirty cop but now had to prove it. It took them over a month but finally put together enough evidence to arrest him.

Miami-Dade police detectives secured a warrant for the arrest of Manny Pardo, charging him with four of the nine homicides he was suspected of being involved in. The Miami Dade County Police asked the

Hialeah Police SWAT Team to execute the search and arrest warrant for Officer Pardo.

At the SWAT briefing, I told the team this could be one of our most dangerous entries as Officer Pardo would be armed in his apartment. Pardo had nothing to lose.

The SWAT Team elected me to be team leader on this arrest. I found an apartment three blocks away from Pardo's residence with the same interior structure and we practiced for an hour prior to assaulting Manny Pardo's residence. We were given the 'go' signal around 2:00 pm in the afternoon.

We got the key to his apartment from Pardo's landlord. I chose my best five-man entry team and stacked outside the front door. I put the key in the deadbolt and, thank God, it turned the cylinder, opening the door.

I decided to go in slow and quiet, rather than hard and fast. I didn't want to turn this into a gun fight.

We swept the house and finally located Manny sleeping on the couch. He was covered by a blanket and had two crutches on the floor next to him. I assumed he might be armed so I moved the blanket and saw a Glock pistol wedged in between him and the couch. I couldn't take the gun out without waking him up.

Hopefully he would not resist if he saw my face. I pointed my Glock Pistol at his head and told Kurt Nagel to wake him up. Nagel grabbed Pardo's foot and shook it. Pardo woke up and looked up and saw three SWAT team members pointing their guns at him. Manny then looked at me, and said, "Shit Wally, what's up!"

I just said, "Manny, I think you know. I really don't want to shoot you now so please put your hands out in front of you. Officer Humberto Valdez handcuffed him. Pardo didn't resist.

Officer Manuel Pardo was convicted on four of the nine homicides, terminated from the Sweetwater Police Department and several years ago, was put to death. He was given a lethal injection on December 11, 2012, by the State of Florida.

8.63 Kill Zone

I remember the night because I was a Rookie on the midnight shift. I was on patrol by myself for maybe three weeks. It was around 11pm when I observed a blue Chevrolet parked next to the Hialeah Hotel. The vehicle's lights were out but the car was running and occupied by four subjects. When they saw me driving up to their location, the two black males in the rear seat ducked down. I could see a lot of movement in the rear seat as if they were covering up something. The driver and passenger both gave me a hard look. We later learned that they were going to rob the hotel manager at gun point.

I pulled in behind them in my marked police car and turned on my overhead blues and red lights. The driver of the car immediately accelerated the vehicle and fled west on Okeechobee Road. I advised dispatch that I was in a 'Chase' on the radio and told them my direction of travel.

We were both driving at a high rate of speed westbound. The car was about thirty yards in front of me when it turned into a residential area. I was not far behind it. After making two turns, the vehicle suddenly stopped and started to turn around. He was making a U-turn.

I stopped at the end of the street, a little confused as to what the vehicle and driver were doing.

The Chevrolet turned around and was driving back towards me. What puzzled me was the car was driving slowly at about 15-20 miles an hour. I put my car in reverse and waited.

The car was about 50-60 feet in front of me heading in my direction. The driver was still driving slowly and that is when I saw him. The rear driver's side passenger had put his window down and was hanging out of the window, holding a sawed off short barreled shotgun with both hands. I could see him clearly. He had a muscular build, no shirt on and was wearing a pair of blue jeans below his belly button. He was now aiming the shotgun at me and my patrol vehicle.

They were going to drive past me and shoot me with the shotgun. I was in the kill zone and needed to move. I backed up as fast as I could. I knew if I could back up fast enough, the shotgun would not be that effective at a greater distance.

I was backing up and they were accelerating. I backed up about fifty feet and turned my wheel and quickly backed into a driveway. Now I was facing the black male holding the shotgun. He was still leaning out of the rear window, pointing the gun in my direction. I backed up some more down the street. Any second, I anticipated him to fire at me. I couldn't defend myself due to the windshield. Again, I was in the kill zone. The only thing I could do was ram him.

I was ready. I couldn't backup, I could only go forward. I got on the radio and quickly advised dispatch of my location and I needed backup. Units had already been dispatched.

At that moment, the subject in the back seat, who was pointing the shotgun at me saw another marked police unit turn the corner. The officer had no idea what had transpired. The black male in the rear seat pulled the shotgun back inside the car and slumped down in the seat so I could not get a good look at him.

They drove past me and the chase was on again. The chase lasted about two minutes until they drove the car into a tree. We ended up arresting three of the four subjects. One of the rear passengers escaped. The car was stolen, the tag was stolen off another vehicle and we recovered the sawed-off shotgun and another handgun.

I had prevented an armed robbery and arrested three dangerous individuals. They all had violent felony backgrounds. With a little luck and lots of skill, I had prevented myself from being killed by the rear passenger with the shotgun.

Kill Zone: Tactical Point

What saved me that night was that I put my car in motion rather than remain stationary as the Chevrolet drove toward me. If I had not moved, you would most likely, not be reading this book. I would have been killed or seriously wounded that night.

The point is that if your car is moving, you are relatively safe. It is when you stop, that you are in danger. Keep moving.

What is the moral of the story? I think you already know. Road rage can kill you. You never know who you are going to enrage while driving. The best advice is to just keep driving without any contact with the other vehicle. As long as you are in motion, you are relatively safe. But, remember, the moment you stop for a red light, stop sign or your car breaks down, your alert levels should automatically be elevated.

8.64 Listen to your Instincts

I was teaching a concealed weapons class and one of the students approached me after class ended. She told me the following story on why she wanted to buy a gun and carry the firearm concealed for protection. She worked for FPL (Florida Power and Light) and lived here in South Florida. Here is the victim's personal story as she told it to me. Let's call her Karen.

The rule after work at FPL had always been that after 5pm, you never go out to the parking lot alone. On this night, Karen was leaving the office a little late and had to go shopping, pick the kids up and make dinner. She left the building alone. It was just getting dark. She just violated the company policy. The time was exactly 5:50pm.

As she hurried to her vehicle, she noticed a middle aged Latin male leaning against the car directly next to hers. He had both arms crossed and she couldn't see his hands. Again, she checked her watch and was running late for the grocery store.

Even though she had that 'gut feeling' and a little voice in her head telling her that something was not right, she still continued walking to her car. Karen made a point to not make eye contact with the unknown male. Her instincts told her to go back inside and get an escort. But, she said to herself, "I'll be ok this time." As she put her key in the car door and opened it, he attacked her.

With lightning speed, he covered the six to eight feet that separated him from her. He put a knife to her throat, forcing her into the car. The subject had concealed a knife under his folded arms. He demanded her car keys and started the engine. He told her, "Move or scream and I will kill you." He then forced her to sit in the passenger seat. He was going to drive.

He drove the car out of the parking lot and went southbound to a school parking lot about a half mile away. Unbeknownst to the attacker, one of her co-workers witnessed the abduction. She called the police.

The armed subject stopped her car in a secluded school parking lot. As he pressed the knife against her neck, he told her, "Cooperate and I won't hurt you. Now pull your panties off." Terrified, she did exactly what he told her to do. The subject had the victim pinned down in her front seat and was raping her. With the knife to her throat, he sexually battered the victim.

Miami-Dade Police issued a BOLO (Be on the lookout) for her vehicle. After about eight minutes, an officer spotted her car in the school lot. As the officer cautiously approached the car from the rear, he could see the male was still raping her with the knife pushed against her throat.

The police officer called for backup and immediately drew his service firearm and ordered the man out of the car. The rapist exited the car with the knife to the victim's throat. He told the police officer, "Get back or I will kill her." The officer could see the victim was only partially clothed and from her appearance, he knew she had been raped.

The police officer was a member of the Miami-Dade Special Response Team and quickly aimed at the head of the rapist and fired once. This is a shot he could make being a SWAT Team officer.

The armed rapist was shot and killed as he held the knife to the victim's throat. She had survived the ordeal but was severely traumatized from the rape and having the rapist shot and killed so close to her face.

This was not going to happen to her again. She was now taking a class to carry a gun for self-defense. She survived the armed sexual battery, but the emotional trauma and mental scars will last forever.

Listen to Your Instincts: Tactical Solution

This tragedy would not have happened if the victim had listened to her instincts. That little voice in her head told her something was wrong. That instinct or feeling that you are in the presence of danger is a three-million year-old instinct. Listen to it!

Secondly, never let the attacker relocate you from where you are. Statistics show that if an attacker relocates his victim, the chances of the victim being killed are more than seventy-five percent.

He knows that the terrible things he wants to do to you cannot be done where you are right now. It's time to fight. Resist; stand your ground and do whatever you have to do. Never let the attacker relocate you. If you do, it will be your worst nightmare.

8.65 Armed Robbery at the Mall

We had been watching this black male for about thirty minutes. His actions were extremely suspicious. He seemed to be waiting for someone. Unknown to us, he had already selected a female target who parked and went into the mall. He was waiting for her to come back to her car.

More time passed and he seemed to get irritated. He walked toward the Burdines entrance, stopped and put something in the flowers. None of us could tell what he put in the flowers but later, we learned, it was a Smith & Wesson .38 caliber revolver. He entered the mall.

After only a few minutes, he came outside, stooped down and picked up the gun from the flower bed. He hurriedly moved back to his car and sat in the vehicle. Less than a minute later, a Latin female exited the mall and walked toward the direction of the black male sitting in his car. Her car was parked very near to his.

As she approached her vehicle, the male got out and ran towards her. When he was about three feet from her, he pulled the revolver from his waistband and put it to her head.

Later, we learned that she was his former girlfriend, and this was more of a domestic than a robbery. They were breaking up and he wanted money and she said, "No." He then, at gun point, forcibly took cash from her purse and a ring from her finger. The entire time he was pointing the gun at the female.

My partner, Tommy Hopkins and I agreed to wait until the robbery was over. We didn't want to make the robbery a hostage situation. After taking her purse and going through her wallet, he threw it at her. He then physically pushed her, pointed the gun at her head and said something but didn't shoot. He turned and walked away.

Once he got into his vehicle, we moved in and attempted to stop him. He fled at a high rate of speed. I gave dispatch the tag number and direction of travel to get help from other marked units. Dispatch advised that the car was stolen. We were both northbound on West 16th Avenue, exceeding 70-80 miles per hour in a residential area.

The subject drove without caution. He was running red lights and caused three separate accidents where he hit other cars and kept going. I was the passenger in an unmarked car with Detective Hopkins. He was driving and I was on the radio.

I was advising dispatch of his direction of travel and all of the accidents he had caused along the way.

Trying to lose us, he increased his speed. The subject driving the stolen vehicle turned westbound on 72nd Street. This was a residential neighborhood. Suddenly, he put his breaks on. The car was moving at about thirty miles an hour. The driver then moved over to the passenger seat. Still trying to steer the car, he opened the passenger side door and jumped out of the moving vehicle. He hit the ground and almost immediately jumped up running.

I yelled, "Hopkins, run him over." He doesn't and now it's a foot chase. The robbery subject's car crashed into a huge oak tree. Hopkins was checking the vehicle and I was behind the subject, running as fast as I could. I am not that fast of a runner. I had my Smith & Wesson 8mm in my hand, but I couldn't get a good shot. I was not sure if he was still armed or not but I was yelling, "Police, stop or I'll shoot!" He ran northbound and jumped into a canal. It was dark and I wasn't sure if he swam across the canal or was hiding in the tall grass.

Other units arrived and we set up a perimeter around the area. I called Miami-Dade County for their helicopter to join in the search. One hour and a half later, we still had not found him. I told all the units to clear. We had lost him. I couldn't believe we lost this armed robbery subject. He either drowned or somehow got out of the perimeter.

The four of us, Hopkins, Poole, Flutie and I were in plain clothes and we met at the Winn Dixie on 68th Street to discuss how in the hell we lost him. This was about four to six blocks from the canal. We were standing in front of a Cuban Café having coffee.

I looked over Sandy's shoulder and there he was; the robbery subject. I could not believe my eyes. He had taken off his shirt and he was drenched from head to toe. The subject from the robbery was walking right towards us. I said to the three other officers, "Don't turn around, but the guy from the mall robbery is right behind you."

One of the guys turned around and the foot chase was on again. Hopkins ran past me and tackled the armed gunman. I jumped on the pile also. Sandy and another officer, Humberto Valdez had their guns out and were covering us in the event the subject still had a gun. Hopkins yelled, "I got you, mother fucker!" With that, he bent this guy's leg over his head. The only problem with that was, that was my leg! I yelled, "Hopkins, that's my leg, you idiot!" Sometimes, in those fights you don't know who's who. My knee hurt for weeks.

We finally got him handcuffed. We arrested him for armed robbery, aggravated assault with a firearm, fleeing a police officer, grand theft auto and all of the traffic accidents offenses. We recovered the firearm from his waistband along with the victim's jewelry and several hundred dollars in cash.

Armed Robbery at the Mall: Learning Point

The above documented criminal activity all occurred in one mall. When you go shopping at a mall, be careful! It's a watering hole for predators.

8.66 Crack Baby

Being assigned to vice and narcotics was exciting. It was something new and different every day. One day, we would work prostitutes, the next day, we would sell drugs and if it was slow, we would do a reverse sting. A reverse sting is when the police sell crack to the addicts and then arrest them for possession.

At the office in the morning, we would conduct intelligence briefing on what kind of activity we had that day in our crack areas, within the city. We would then pick a location to do reverse stings and sell crack and arrest the buyers. The first thing we did was to send in an undercover police officer to make a buy from the drug dealer on the corner. Once he or she bought the crack, they would leave and within minutes, we would arrest the crack seller and confiscate all their cocaine. We then put an undercover police officer at the same location, selling crack to addicts.

The crack addicts come to the area 24/7/365 to purchase crack cocaine. Most arrive by car but some walk, take cabs or friends bring them. When they approach the undercover police officer, the buyer has to tell him what they want. The court ruled that we cannot entice the buyer to purchase crack when they ordinarily wouldn't have.

For example, the undercover (UC) officer stands on the corner where the other seller was. The crack buyers approach him and say, "You selling?" The UC responds back, "What do you want?" The buyer will then ask, "How much?" The seller will then say something like, "Twenty each." That's when the buyer will say, "I'll take two rocks." The UC officer is wearing a wire and we can hear and tape record the entire transaction.

Sometimes, the buyer wants to pick out his or her own rocks. So, the seller will show them to the buyer, and they will pick out two good-sized cocaine rocks. Once the buyer takes possession of the rocks, the signal is given for the takedown team to move in and arrest the buyer. He or she is then charged with purchasing and possession of a controlled substance, to wit; cocaine.

One particular day, a woman in her late twenties arrived by a taxi with a baby. She got out and went up to the UC and said, "I can't take care of my baby anymore. I will give him to you for eight rocks."

The UC stepped to the side and raised me on the radio. He said, "Sarge, you won't believe this. She wants to trade her baby for eight rocks."

Sergeant Philbrick, "Ask her how old the baby is." He came back on the radio and said, "Four months. It's a boy." I thought for a second and said, "Offer her four rocks and see what she will do." I was parked about fifty yards away in an unmarked van.

The UC officer walked back over to the woman and was seen conversing with her as she held the baby. After a minute, I saw the mother kiss her baby goodbye and hand the infant to the UC officer. She must have taken the agreed upon four rocks from him, turned and got in the cab and drove away.

He told me, as she was driving away, "I gave her six rocks. She wouldn't take four. I have her four-month old son. What do we do with the baby?"

I had a marked police unit stop the taxi and I pulled up to where they were selling crack. The UC officer was holding the baby and handed the baby to me as I walked up. I opened the soft blue blanket to see the child. He was awake, a little dirty but appeared healthy. The mother was brought back to the scene in handcuffs. I approached her and asked her why she sold her baby. She stated, "I just couldn't take care of him anymore. I've got nobody. I'm homeless, got no job and I'm a crack whore. Fine parent I make."

I just looked her in the eyes and said, "Don't worry, we will take good care of your baby. Does he have a name?" She replied, "His name is Alexander. Alexander Rogers."

After arresting Rebecca Rogers and having Child Services pick up her baby, the UC officer continued selling crack to more than eighty additional buyers for the next four hours. We were so busy processing arrests, we had to put the prisoners in an empty pool at the community center that was being repaired. In five hours, we sold over two-hundred crack rocks and arrested more than ninety people.

We had to shut it down. Business was just too good. We were just too busy selling crack, doing takedowns, impounding the rocks and filling out affidavits. We could have arrested another fifty buyers if we had the manpower.

One of my guys asked me, "Hey Sarge, do we do a property receipt for the baby?" I didn't have an answer for him.

Crack Baby: Tactical Point

It takes a lot of interdepartmental coordination to conduct a drug sting. You need a lot of people for the takedowns, processing, money, inventory of crack, marked units, etc. Plan ahead; because nothing ever goes as planned.

8.67 Reverse Sting: Pizza and Crack

Our biggest drug problem area in Hialeah, Florida was Seminola. These street corner vendors would sell more than $15,000 in crack in one day. When the drug problem got out of hand we would conduct a reverse sting. A reverse sting is when we arrest the crack sellers and put undercover police officers on the corner selling drugs. The concept is arrest all the buyers and there would be no drug problem.

The paperwork involved in making 80 arrests and impounding the cash, vehicles, property, buyers and crack is huge. Every arrest is a minimum of three to four reports. It's a lot of work and is a total team effort.

After one of our stings, Sergeant Finley told everyone "Free pizza and beer for doing a good job. Meet at the parking lot just north of the station." There is a large parking lot there with benches and shade trees.

After all the prisoners were processed, crack impounded and money counted, about fifteen of us met for pizza on Sergeant Findley, or was it?

We met at the lot and about twenty minutes later, Sgt. Finley arrived with the ice cold beer and ten pizzas. Everyone was eating pizza and enjoying a cold beer after working all day.

Now, I was no Rookie, so I was thinking how in the hell did he get police administration to pay for an after sting pizza party? My guess, the cost would be around $150. To get the city to pay for that would take an act of God. I was wondering how he got the city to pay for this. He didn't.

I was a sergeant at the time. I got Sgt. Finley alone and said, "Arnold, it's nice of you to pay for the pizza and beer. I just wanted to thank you. I know it wasn't cheap."

Arnold looked at me, paused and said, "Son, I didn't pay for this, the city of Hialeah did."

Confused and puzzled, I asked Finley, "How did you get the City of Hialeah to pay? It's got to be over a $150."

Arnold looked at me and whispered, "I used the profit from the crack sales to pay for the pizza and beer. Keep that to yourself, Philbrick."

I loved Sgt. Finley's motivation and effort to thank the police officers who worked the sting but that would never happen today. Today, every dollar and piece of crack is counted and impounded by more than one responsible officer.

Pizza and Crack: Financial Point

More than one person should be responsible for the inventory of anything of value, especially crack and cash. It's just good business.

Next time, before the sting begins, ask the supervisors to pitch in and help pay for the 'after sting' party.

8.68 One More Sale

This story is unbelievable, but it shows what a crack addict will do for the drug.

The Narcotics and Vice Unit conducted a lot of drug stings to combat the sale of crack and cocaine in Hialeah. Most of the narcotics guys were SWAT team members so we would bring the SWAT truck once the operation was over. The SWAT truck was just a big bread truck with seats and cabinets. The entry door was exactly like a school bus.

On this particular night, we were in the SWAT truck, counting the money to match it to how many rocks we sold. Everyone was in SWAT fatigues and wore police radios, handcuff cases, side arms, badges, police hats, etc.

All of a sudden, there was a knock on the glass entry door to the truck. It was a crack user looking for dope. As he was banging on the door, he yelled, "Can I get two?"

I told Officer Jim Poole to tell him to come back tomorrow, the store was closed. Poole yelled at the crack guy, "Get out of here." The guy turned and walked away. A minute later, he was back at the door. Poole opened the door.

In the SWAT van, are nine police officers all wearing their guns and tactical gear. Everyone was trying to hide their guns from this crazy ass crack hound banging on the bi-fold door.

He stepped into the van and said, "Can I get two? I know I'm late."

Officer Jimmy Somohano yelled at the guy, "Get the fuck out, don't you know who we are?"

He responded, "I don't care who you are. Now sell me two rocks." We couldn't believe this asshole was still trying to buy two rocks from us after we just arrested more than ninety people. I said, "Jimmy, sell him two."

Somohano had to go to the back of the van and get two crack rocks while the buyer stood there looking at all of us. I was thinking he must think we are some kind of football team or something.

Somohano handed him the two rocks and said, "Twenty dollars." The buyer looked at the rocks and said, "Wow, these are good size rocks, give me one more." I couldn't believe this.

I yelled to Somohano, "Jimmy, get our money." The guy handed the detective two ten-dollar bills and stood there waiting for the other rock. I said, "Jimmy, '39' him. In police code, that means to arrest him.

Somohano took out his handcuffs and cuffed the buyer's wrist as he said, "Sir, you are under arrest for possession of cocaine."

The purchaser was stunned that he was going to jail for buying two rocks. I guess reality set in finally.

One More Sale: Narcotics Addiction

People on crack cocaine or heroin live in a fog. All they care about is getting that narcotic. The need for that drug was so strong, he didn't care that we were the police. His desire for crack was all he thought about, regardless of the circumstances. Remember that when you are dealing with someone hooked on a drug.

8.69 The Bum and the Dumpster

I was working in the SWAT-Tac unit in plain clothes. We would work different areas if a particular crime surfaced in that area. This night, we were conducting static surveillance for commercial burglaries of warehouses and businesses.

When working warehouse burglaries, you have to outsmart the bad guys. You have to be in a position where you can see them, but they can't see you. I've sat in wrecked cars, on roof tops, in the business itself, in trees and more. It was a cold night for South Florida and I wanted to stay warm, so I got into a dumpster in front of a warehouse.

It took me a few minutes to set up my cardboard so I wouldn't get too dirty. After that, I waited. It was about 1:30am. I was sitting in a relatively clean dumpster with the top lid propped up about a foot, so I could see. It was warm in the dumpster compared to outside. I was in radio contact with three other officers as we waited.

They were all around the block, behind a warehouse, drinking coffee in their heated plain clothes cars. Will Perez was on the roof and complaining about how cold it was.

I'm in the dumpster and Perez raises me on the radio. He whispers, "Single white male walking southbound at East 11th and 24th." I peeked out of the dumpster and the unknown male was walking in my direction. I slowly unsnapped my Glock pistol and took it out of the holster. I got as deep as I could in the dumpster and moved to one side. I could no longer see the suspect walking in my direction.

I had my ear-piece in and Perez whispered, "Philbrick, he's walking in your direction." I couldn't see him but I had my Glock pistol in my hand. I didn't know if he was a burglar, a bum or just some guy walking home from work.

Suddenly, the dumpster lid opened, and the male jumped into the dumpster, almost landing on top of me. It scared the hell out of me. The lieutenant and other guys watched and were all laughing. They knew he was a bum and not a burglar.

It was dark and I really couldn't see him. I didn't know if he was armed or not. When he jumped in his leg hit my shoulder. He yelled, "What are you doing in my dumpster?" Trying to keep my police identity secret, I responded, "I was cold." He barked, "Get the hell out, this is my dumpster." I holstered my gun and climbed out of the dumpster, as he said, "Go find your own dumpster."

I was so glad I didn't shoot him. I just walked away and raised the lieutenant on the radio to come pick me up. I could have been killed while my team was enjoying my misadventure.

I couldn't have been more tactical that night. Plan on the unexpected and have a backup plan. 'Shit happens."

8.70 The Cock Fight

The sport of cockfighting in Hialeah was very popular. Two male roosters would fight to the death. This was a sport in Cuba and the game rekindled in South Florida. Hundreds of spectators would meet secretly in a make-shift arena and bring their birds to fight. Thousands of dollars were waged on each cock fight. It is a brutal sport where in the end, one of the chickens dies or is close to death. The birds combat each other until one of them can no longer fight. Usually, the losing chicken is thrown in a trash can to die.

One night, Office Sandra Saint Germain was dispatched to a cockfight. You have to get to know Sandy. She's old school but likes to play with the system. Here is a small part of the narrative from one of her police reports.

Officer Saint Germain's police report:

"Upon arrival, this officer observed more than sixty men standing around an open arena. Two of the men were standing in the middle of the ring, holding their cocks in their hands. I looked at both cocks and noticed that one of them was bigger than the other one. I had never in my life seen a cock that big. The head and neck were stiff and erect. The shorter of the two men possessed the smaller cock. He was holding his cock in his right hand. His cock appeared lifeless and limp. On the head of his cock I could see blood and other unknown fluids. He was rubbing the head of his cock, but it wasn't responding. Officer St Germain approached him and said, "Whose cock is that?" He replied, "This cock is mine." Then she asked, "What's wrong with your cock?" He replied, "I can't get it to stay up." Germain then asked, "Why won't your cock stay up?" He replied, "I think it's tired. It got beat up pretty bad." Saint Germain looked at the other man and asked, "Why are you holding your cock in your hand?" Unknown Latin male replied, "I was just playing with it." Saint Germain, "Why are you playing with your cock at midnight out here in the woods?" He replied, "It's the only cock I have.""

I think you get the gist of how the report was worded. Police administration put the report through because it was what she witnessed upon arrival. She just used some words that could mean two different things. Everyone got a good laugh out of her report. Thank you, Sandy, for a little bit of humor on the job.

8.71 The Shoplifter

I was working patrol and was dispatched to the Burdines store at our local mall. Burdines security was holding a shoplifter they caught stealing clothes.

When I arrived, I met with the security director and he said, "We have been trying to catch this guy for a long time. He has been stealing from this store for several months. He's been killing us."

While I was interviewing the security manager, the subject, who they caught shoplifting was yelling at me, "It's just a misdemeanor, officer. The value is not over three hundred dollars.

In Florida, any theft under $300 is a misdemeanor. That amount would be $299.99 and below. Any theft of $300 or more is grand theft and a felony. A felony conviction could mean jail time for more than a year.

If this thief was arrested and had a valid Florida Driver's License, most police agencies PTA the shoplifter. A PTA is where the offender is released on the scene, they sign the arrest form and PTA (promise to appear in court). You can't PTA a felony charge.

This shoplifter lived in Hialeah and was not a flight risk. He would most likely show up in court. But, this guy needed to go to jail. This was the second time he was stopped by security at Burdines. This time, they found him with the merchandise and the items he was stealing. He was stopped as he tried to leave the store.

We took the two bags of clothes he had stolen and started adding them up. I wanted to see what the total amount of his theft was. Meanwhile, the offender was telling me, "Hey, officer, the total value is $285.00 exactly. I kept a running total. It's under $300. It's still a misdemeanor."

It always amazes me that these criminals know the law as good as or better than most police officers. He knew if he kept his total theft under $300, it would remain a misdemeanor and he would be released.

We totaled up the two bags of stolen clothing and yes, he was right. The value was exactly $285.00.

The Burdines security director was disappointed that we could not put him in jail. Meanwhile, the thief, Rafael Gonzalez said, "Where do I sign, I want to get out of here."

I thought for a second and looked Mr. Gonzalez in the eyes and said,

"Sir, you forgot one thing." The thief asked, "What is that, officer? It was under $300, let me sign and leave."

I replied, "Not so fast Mr. Gonzalez."

Here you have a professional thief that knows the law and thinks he is going to walk after getting caught stealing hundreds of dollars of merchandise. This guy needs to go to jail. I thought for a minute and walked over to where the subject, Rafael Gonzalez was standing.

I said, "Mr. Gonzalez, when you were stealing the Burdines merchandise, you forgot about one thing."

He looked at me with that 'puppy dog' look and said, "What did I forget, officer?"

I replied, "You didn't factor in the 6% sales tax on your purchase....I mean, theft."

Gonzales asked, "How much is sales tax?"

The security director got out a calculator and smiled and looked at me and said, "Six percent on $285.00 is $17.10. That makes it a total of $302.10."

I turned to Mr. Gonzalez and smiled as I said, "Put your hands behind your back. You re under arrest for grand theft."

8.72 The Duck

One afternoon, in patrol, I was dispatched to an animal abuse call in zone one. When I arrived, the secondary patrol unit had a white male in custody. He was an American male in his 20's. He was wearing blue shorts and a pair of sneakers. He had no shirt on and was wet from head to toe.

I asked the other officer, "What do we have?" He replied, "This guy was fucking that duck," as he pointed to a dead duck on a picnic table. The duck was your typical white duck with orange feet. It was pretty big. I walked over and nudged it. It didn't move. The duck was dead.

Just then, a Latin female in her 60's said in broken English, "He was having sex with that duck"

I called for a supervisor to respond to our location.

I interviewed the witness and she said, "That man chased the duck in and out of the lake until he caught him. Then he pulled his pants down and held the duck still with both hands and screwed the duck. I couldn't see his penis. I think it was small. I think he killed the duck with his penis."

I walked over to the handcuffed prisoner and said, "What is your name?" He replied, "Ronnie Lasik." I asked him, "Did you kill that duck?" He replied, "I fucked it, but I didn't mean to kill it."

At that time, a sergeant arrived on scene and requested ID to take photographs of the dead duck and the subject who still had feathers in his underwear. After doing the paperwork, I transported Ronnie Lasik to the main jail.

About three weeks later, I received a subpoena to attend court. I had to appear in court and testify about what I observed. I was sitting about two rows behind the defendant, Ronnie Lasik waiting to testify. I just couldn't help myself. We were both waiting for his case to be called.

I started quietly making the sound of a duck, "quack, quack, quack." Then I changed it to a happy sounding duck. After that, I made the sound of a satisfied duck, "Quaaaack, quaaaack…….." I got Ronnie's attention and he kept looking at me. We were in the back of the court room where the judge couldn't hear me.

After a few minutes Ronnie Lasik turned around and looked at me and whispered, "Best pussy I ever had."

The court found him guilty of animal cruelty and fined him $250 and thirty hours of community service.

In my police career, I never encountered someone who had intercourse with a duck except 'Ronnie, the duck fucker.'

8.73 Hurricane Warning

I was on the departmental task force for hurricane preparation and post storm clean-up. Prior to a hurricane hitting South Florida, we would meet and formulate a hurricane preparedness plan and put our department on the Alpha Bravo shift. Everyone works twelve-hour shifts. The goal is to have everyone in the city sleeping at the police and/or fire stations or hotels. After a major hurricane, getting to work was totally impossible for days after a storm.

Several years ago, South Florida issued a hurricane warning. Hurricane Andrew was a fast moving, category 4 storm that was just east of Miami and moving west towards the coast. A category 4 storm predicates knocking down most concrete walls, downing large trees and destroying every trailer.

Hialeah had two fairly large trailer parks, both with more than seventy trailers. We were assigned the task of going out to each trailer, trying to get the residents to evacuate prior to the storm hitting. They didn't want to leave. Most of the residents believed their trailer could withstand a major hurricane. After a meeting, we changed our tactics on getting residents to leave.

With another officer in uniform, we would knock on the door of a trailer. The occupant would come out and we would tell them, "A dangerous category 4 storm is due to hit South Florida in the next six to ten hours. We need you to evacuate to a shelter that the city has set up at Milander Park." The resident, in most cases would say, "This is my home and I'm not leaving."

I would reiterate that a category 4 storm has major flooding and winds over 135 miles per hour. "We highly recommend you evacuate to the shelter." They would say, "No thank you, officer, we are going to ride out the storm in our trailer."

That is when I would say, "Would you do me a favor?" They would reply, "Sure, how can I help you?" I would then ask them, "Can you please extend your right arm and pull up your sleeve?" When I said that, the other officer would reach into his pocket and take out a big black permanent magic marker. The resident, a little confused, would say, "What is that for?" I would then tell them, "The officer is going to write your social security number on your arm with the marker. It will be readable on your arm for a few days."

Confused, and a bit bewildered, the resident would ask, "Why?" My response was, "When we find your body floating in the canal, it will make identifying your corpse a little easier."

You should have seen their faces. After a few seconds, most of the trailer residents would say, "Where is that shelter again?"

Hurricane Warning: Tactical Point

Listen to the weather reports and respond accordingly. Hurricanes change course in a minute. An hour ago, you were out of danger, but now the eye is moving in your direction and you have no place to go.

Hurricane preparation begins before June 1st and not when you are in a hurricane warning. Plan ahead.

8.74 Whoops, Sorry, Didn't Mean It

In Hialeah, we had a drug infested area called Seminola. Everyone in the neighborhood was selling crack. They had children on street corners alerting the drug dealers when the police were arriving. Our narcotics team would move in on a regular basis and arrest the drug dealer and put an undercover police officer on the corner selling crack.

I was on the takedown team. The undercover police officer would give the signal that the drug deal was over, he had the crack money and the buyer had the $10 piece of crack. When the transaction was over, the undercover (UC) officer would take his hat off. That was our signal to move in and arrest the buyer.

One evening, we were all set up, waiting for a deal to go down. A Camaro pulled up and the UC officer, Perez walked over to the driver's door. The driver was a white male. I had a good visual of the driver and the officer. It was dark so I couldn't see the actual deal go down. After a minute, the UC officer stepped back, scratched his head and took his cap off.

We moved in. The takedown team was made up of four officers. Two officers with handguns covered the takedown team who removed the subject out of the vehicle. I reached in and grabbed the driver who had just bought the crack, as the other officer opened the door. He resisted me so I forcibly knocked him to the ground. He hit the pavement hard, screaming. I told him, "Be quiet, you are under arrest for possession and purchase of cocaine, a controlled substance."

Willie Perez, the UC officer looked at me and said, "Philbrick, what are you doing?" I responded, "How many rocks did he buy?" He leaned over and quietly said to me, "Wally, what the fuck are you doing? The guy didn't buy anything."

It was an 'Oh Shit moment.' I was on top of the driver with my knee on his shoulder. He was handcuffed, face down. Then, the subject said to me, "I didn't buy anything."

I looked at the UC and said, "You gave the signal, didn't you?" Perez looked at me and said, "Shit, I scratched my head and I may have taken my cap off for a second." That's when I knew we fucked up. We just arrested, handcuffed and forcibly took down a man who didn't commit a crime.

I asked the UC what the man wanted or said when he had approached the driver's door? He said, "He was lost and wanted directions to the mall."

Lt. Beyer came over and took the handcuffs off the driver of the vehicle. He took the driver to the side and explained what we were doing there. Beyer physically wiped the driver off and put his hand out to shake hands with the driver. The driver slowly met Beyer's hand and shook it. The driver got in his car and left.

Lt. Beyer walked over and told us, "Next time you give the fucking signal, make sure it's a buy. That guy was a little pissed off but understood what we were doing. I think we are ok."

The victim of our police brutality didn't complain because he was most likely there to score a rock and lied about being lost. We tightened up our takedown signal and went on to arrest ninety-three people that day. Selling crack in Seminola was like shooting fish in a barrel.

8.75 Kind of Smoking Marijuana on Duty

It was my second year on the force, when the narcotics division confiscated over two tons of marijuana from a drug deal. The bales of marijuana completely filled a tractor trailer.

The trial was over, and I was part of a twenty-man rolling security team. Under tight security, we moved the hundred plus bales of marijuana from city hall to a vacant lot near the patrol building.

Right next to the police station, on Lejeune Road, was a couple acres of land. During weekends, the land was used for a flea market. With tight security and marijuana worth millions of dollars, we arrived at the city owned land next to the police department. Prior to our arrival, bull dozers had dug two large pits to burn and bury the marijuana.

I was security and watched the narcotics agents cut the bales up so they could burn them. After a few hours, both pits were almost full. There was maybe two or three feet of space from the marijuana to ground level.

By now, more than fifty people had arrived and were watching. Some of them were standing on dirt mounds from the holes the city dug. One of the detectives went to his vehicle and brought out a can of gasoline and started pouring it on the marijuana in the holes. He saturated most of the bales and lit it on fire.

Minutes later, the crowd of fifty people or more were cheering. I knew why. I was standing next to one of the pits, downwind. The smoke had me higher than a kite and the wind was moving this marijuana cloud westerly, where the crowd of people were all standing. Everyone was getting high.

After the Chief realized what was happening, one of the Captains got on the bull horn and told all the civilians they had to leave. Reluctantly, and as slow as possible, the now seventy-five plus bystanders were leaving. Meanwhile, I and about ten other officers, still downwind, were getting high from the burning. After about three hours, the burn was over, or some thought. We all went home.

I came to work the next morning for the 8am roll call. When I drove past the burned marijuana pits, I noticed there was green and brown pot everywhere. I parked and walked over to the pit.

Both marijuana pits contained clean unburned marijuana. The fire had just burned the top, maybe three to four feet deep and under that was clean, unburned marijuana. The gasoline had saturated just a few feet deep and burned that weed only. Under that, maybe ten feet deeper, was clean, unburned marijuana.

The Chief quickly placed a marked unit there to ward off any more diggers. Later in the morning, city workers arrived and dug out both pits and put the weed in large boxes like a refrigerator would fit in. The drugs were then transported to an incinerator in North Florida and burned again. The city did not want this on the evening news.

Nice job, Chief. The locals appreciated the 'love-in.'

8.76 Surviving a Gunshot Wound to the Head

On April 15, 1980, the United States agreed to let Cubans immigrate to the United States. Over one-hundred twenty-five thousand men, women, children immigrated to the United States. What the United States didn't count on was that Castro emptied his prisons sending all his mentally ill, rapists, robbers, and violent criminals to Florida. The first thing these criminals did was get a gun.

After the Cuban Mariel Boatlift crime in Hialeah was out of control. Miami Dade County police and Hialeah doubled their homicides in one year. I was dispatched to a robbery-shooting. Upon arrival, I observed the injured victim from the armed robbery standing in the front of a business. His face was covered with blood and fire rescue had just arrived to treat him. He shot in the head by his attacker. He was being robbed at gun point and had resisted.

The robbery subject shot him once in the forehead with a .22 caliber revolver. The bullet hit his forehead and punctured the skin but not his cranium. The bullet traveled on a slight angle and then hit his skull, which was unusually thick. The victim was from Cuba and after spending ten years in prison, thought being shot was not a big deal. Luckily for him, the shooter shot him at an angle and the bullet actually travelled completely around his skull, inside the skin around his head. Remarkably, he was not seriously injured. Had the bullet been of higher caliber, it would have penetrated his skull and most likely killed him.

Having this type of gunshot wound and surviving, is more common than you think. If you get shot and you are still standing and alive, it's a good sign. Unless you are shot in the head or spinal cord, you will still be able to function. You may have a survivable gunshot wound. Do not fall to the ground. One of our first reactions when we are shot is to fall to the ground. When we're children playing cops and robbers, we fall to the ground when we are shot. We learned this reaction as children. The key is to minimize your injuries so you can continue fighting.

Surviving a Gunshot Wound to the Head: Survival Point

If you are shot, that doesn't mean you are going to die. If your life is in danger, become the aggressor and attacker. This might surprise your attacker enough that he might flee. If you have a chance for survival, take it and never give up.

8.77 Racetrack Stabbing

I was a patrol officer working the afternoon shift. I was dispatched to the Hialeah Racetrack. The call was dispatched first as an injured person. Shortly thereafter, dispatch advised that someone had been stabbed.

Upon arrival, I met a horse trainer named Pepe Suarez, who had gotten into a knife fight with another trainer. Obviously, he had lost the knife fight. His pants and shirt were drenched in blood. He had been slashed across his stomach with a very sharp knife. The knife wound had cut his stomach wide open. He was doing a pretty good job of holding his intestines inside the wound. He kept tucking his intestines back into his stomach. He was in a lot of pain but very conscious and alert.

I told him to sit down and apply mild pressure to his stomach. By having him sit down, it took pressure off his stomach and helped seal the knife wound. Fire rescue responded and taped up his stomach prior to transporting him to the hospital.

Racetrack Stabbing: Survival Point

First rule of a knife fight or attack. You are going to get cut. Plan on it bu try to minimize your cuts to areas where veins or arteries are not exposed.

If you are attacked, try to keep the knife wounds on your hands, arms and legs. Remember you have exposed arteries underneath your arms. Defend with your forearms. In most cases, you can survive.

If you have time, one self-defense technique is to take your shoes off and put them on your hands. Great for punching and better for protection against a sharp knife.

8.78 Knocking Down the Giant

When I entered the police academy, I was twenty-six years old. I had been doing judo for about eight years and had earned my second-degree black belt from time in grade and competition. I fought in two or three tournaments each month, somewhere in Florida or the United States. Everyone knew I trained in competitive judo.

It was towards the last month of the academy and the defensive tactics trainer, Sergeant Rock wanted to see which police cadets could defend themselves and who couldn't. They would put all the police trainees in a big circle and make us fight each other.

Sergeant Rock would identify one or two of the cadets as police officers. He would then pick a large police cadet and tell the police officer to 'arrest the individual.' The two cadets would usually subdue the 'bad guy' and handcuff him.

After a while, it was my turn in the circle. They paired me up with John Van Rider. Trainee, Van Rider was a giant of a man. He was 6'8" tall and weighed close to 275 pounds. I was less than 180 pounds. Sergeant Rock yelled out, "Philbrick, arrest Van Rider."

I grabbed trainee, Van Rider and tried to control him standing up. He was too big and strong for me to get handcuffs on him when he was standing up. Just about that time, a police captain, watching, yelled out, "Come on, Philbrick, show us some judo." I knew if I used a judo throw on Van Rider, he might get hurt. Then, the Captain yelled out again, "Philbrick, arrest him." I had no choice.

I grabbed trainee Van Rider with my competitive judo grip and moved in for a judo throw. I threw him with one of my best competition techniques which was a leg sweep.

Van Rider, big as he was, hit the ground hard with me on top of him. When he hit the ground, I moved in to handcuff him. That's when he screamed and I knew he was injured. I had dislocated his right shoulder when I threw him.

I had downed a giant, but I felt small because I hurt one of my fellow police trainees. Van Rider went to the ER for x-rays and I went to lunch. The x-rays showed he had a fractured collar bone. Thankfully, the academy let him graduate with our class even though he couldn't perform a lot of the remaining defensive tactics techniques.

Van Rider worked for the Homestead Police Department for over twenty-five years and retired in 2004. Everyone should learn how to defend themselves, whether you are a police officer or a civilian.

I went on to have a pretty good competitive judo career. I made the rank of six degree black belt in 2019 and had competed in hundreds of judo tournaments. I won the World Police and Fire Games and the United States Masters several times.

8.79 Trapped and Dead

I was the Police Department's SWAT Team Training Coordinator for ten years and developed most of the training that kept our team safe, sharp and deadly. Every month or so, we would find an abandoned building scheduled for destruction and go in and just tear it up.

We would use stun grenades, tear down doors, rappel through windows, and use positive entries-explosives that destroyed the door so the team could make entry.

On this particular day, I found an old abandoned hotel on Miami Beach that was going to be leveled in about sixty days. It was perfect for the day's training.

We were practicing slow searches and were looking for a bad guy hiding in a room, closet, stairs or attic. We finished a few scenarios when SWAT Team Officers, Kurt Nagel and Dennis Kerrigan asked me, "Do you smell that?" I said, "Smell what?"

Officer Willie Perez turned and started sniffing the air and left the room. He was following his nose. Suddenly, he cried out, "Sarge, get in here."

I went through three rooms and entered a hallway where Perez and Nagel were standing. Both men were looking up.

I got to where they were standing and immediately looked up. The upper wood floor had rotted and there was a body wedged in between the floorboards. The person was dead.

The deceased male was wearing a pair of shorts with a white t-shirt and one shoe. Obviously, he fell from above, got wedged in the floorboards and couldn't get out. His skin was mummified from the sun. He had been there at least two to three weeks for the sun to dry out his skin, almost leather-like. What a terrible way to die. He must have died a horrible death. How many days did he scream for help?

We called the Miami Beach Police and they handled the investigation of the dead body.

8.80 The Miracle Bullet

By now, you know that I practiced judo and some karate. I became friends with a martial artist named Carlos Montolvo who practiced karate and a little judo. He fought in the police Olympics and always won the gold medal. Carlos came to my judo club a few times and we became good friends. Oh, I forgot to mention that Carlos was also an ATF (Alcohol, Tobacco and Firearms) Agent.

Special Agent Montolvo and the Hialeah Police were jointly working a cocaine dealer for over three months. The Feds would always include the municipality for support. On this day, Carlos was on the phone with the dealer and he told Carlos he had a few extra kilos of cocaine and some guns that he would sell for a low price.

This was the first time that Carlos and the Hialeah Police purchased quantity together. Anytime you buy drugs or guns and the exchange is for tens of thousands of dollars in cash, there is always the chance the deal is a rip off.

To make it a little safer, Carlos told the seller to meet him in the northwest parking lot of the Westland Mall. In the event the deal turned sour, there were less pedestrians or shoppers nearby. That part of the mall backed into a canal and the expressway. A perfect spot for a drug deal or a gun fight.

A lot of times, when you conduct a large drug deal, the seller wants to move the buy location, sometimes two or three times. Lieutenant Doug Faulk told Carlos at the briefing, "Make sure they bring the stuff, we are not going to relocate." Carlos assured the lieutenant they were bringing four kilos of cocaine and a few guns valued at around $150,000. Agent Montalvo told the seller he would bring the cash.

The Lieutenant didn't want to risk being ripped off for the $150,000 in cash, so he decided just to take the sellers down and arrest them. If they didn't have the coke, at least we had conspiracy to sell cocaine.

At 2pm, the sellers arrived in two cars. One was a white Ford and the other a gray Buick. Both cars parked at the northwest corner of the mall. The sellers had arrived, but in two separate vehicles.

We had a spotter on the top of Burdines who confirmed that the sellers had arrived. The Lieutenant gave the order to take them down. Four unmarked vehicles targeted the gray Buick and the Ford. Two marked police units followed the vehicles in, so a police presence was on scene. The passenger in the Buick immediately started shooting at the police.

Carlos Montalvo got out of his car and pointed his gun at the driver of the Ford. Carlos was moving forward while the driver was still sitting in his seat. He appeared to be giving up. Meanwhile, the passenger was killed by Officer Kellogg.

The driver, William Morales, suddenly had a gun and fired at the undercover police officer approaching him from the front of the Ford. Carlos approached the driver's door and noticed the window was up. He was less than five feet from the vehicle. Within a mill-a-second, Morales turned and shot the ATF Agent, Montalvo through the closed window.

Carlos went down as other officer's shot and killed Morales. Agent Montalvo was on the ground with small cuts from the glass shards from the window exploding after Morales shot at him.

Lying on the ground, Carlos conducted a quick assessment of where and if he had been shot. The bullet shot by the assailant should have struck Carlos in the chest; it didn't. Where was the bullet? A quick check of Montalvo's firearm showed the gun had jammed for some reason. The bullet was lodged in the barrel of Carlos Montalvo's Glock pistol.

The 8mm round, fired by Morales, hit the barrel of Montalvo's Glock pistol, shearing off part of the bullet that hit Montalvo. But a majority of the round was now lodged in the barrel of his gun. A miracle had just occurred.

On that day, Carlos wore a shirt much like Jesus would have worn in the old days. He told me on the sting, he looked more like Jesus than an undercover ATF Agent. He was not injured from the partial round that hit him in the chest. His barrel captured the major part of the 8mm round. Hel felt lucky to be alive.

ATF Agent Carlos Montalvo transferred to Puerto Rico four years later and got into another shootout there. Agent Montalvo is alive and well today. Thank God.

His gun is on display in Washington DC at the ATF Headquarters.

8.81 You're No Girl

The 20th Street Bar in Hialeah was where the 'girls' were. Dressed in provocative evening dresses, they stood out in front of the bar and flashed their breasts and flagged down single men in cars. When the men would stop to talk to these 'exotic women,' they were told, "Oral sex for forty dollars cash."

On this night, we were working vice and narcotics. We usually didn't care about hookers and whores until we got a complaint. Then it became a priority and we were told to do something about it. Selling sex was a 24-hour business. There was never a shortage of buyers.

We were about a block away from the bar with binoculars, videotaping part of the solicitation or just watching in amazement at the number of men that would stop and let the prostitute get in their car. At one time there would be three to four girls out front trying to get business. The deal was consummated before she got in the car.

She would instruct him (the John) to drive around the block and park in a dark area behind one of the warehouses. These girls looked good for a few minutes. Conversations were short and the 'john' was directed to a dark corner of a street. That was when you started to question who they really were. The less light when they go to work on the 'johns,' the better.

That night I was with Dennis Kerrigan. We were the takedown team. We always gave the loving couple a few minutes to engage in the act of sex before we pulled up and activated our blues.

We were watching a Cadillac that parked just minutes ago. Dennis and I arrived behind the white Cadillac that was parked next to a clothing warehouse. I hit the lights on our unmarked car and suddenly, I could see two heads pop up, not just one. I always gave one of them a chance to pull his pants up.

We got the 'john' who was usually married, out of the car. Kerrigan got the female out. It was always best to separate the driver from the lady in the evening dress.

The conversation went something like this:

Sgt. Philbrick, "Sir, what are you doing back in the warehouse district at 4:00 am in the morning?"

Male 'john,' "Uh, we were just talking and getting to know each other."

Sgt. Philbrick, "So you know her. What's her name?"

Male John, "I just met her. I don't know her name yet."

Now, Dennis and I know 'her' and her name was Trixie. We had dealt with her before.

Dennis Kerrigan as Trixie, "What were you doing back here in the warehouses?"

Trixie answered in a voice the 'john' had not heard before. She said, in a deep, husky voice, "I'm not going to lie to you. I was giving him head."

I looked at the 'john' and asked him, "Is that correct?"

He replied, "Yes, officer, that is correct."

Sgt. Philbrick, "Sir, did you know Trixie is not a girl, but a man?"

Male 'john,' "No, that's impossible. I felt her down there. It's real."

Note: To make more money when they dress in drag, the male prostitutes will bind their testicles and penis together. They then tie a string around their package and pull it between their legs and tie them off with a string around their waists. From the front, it looks like a woman and feels like one. No matter where you put it, it's still a penis.

The 'john' then says, "There is no law against being with a woman in your own car."

Philbrick, "Sir that is not a woman."

Male 'john,' "I know a woman when I see one. I'm not gay."

Philbrick, "Trixie, show him your dick."

Trixie, "If I do, are you still going to arrest me?"

Philbrick, "No, I won't. But I don't want to see you again."

Trixie pulled down his pants and out pops a 6" penis. The male 'john' leaned over his car and started vomiting.

I told Trixie to get the hell out of here. She sashayed away, walking slowly in the direction of the bar. The white male 'john' finished vomiting and asked me, "Are you going to arrest me?"

I looked at my partner, Officer Kerrigan and he gave me the thumbs down, which meant to let him go. We gave the 'john' a warning and sent him off to his wife and family.

8.82 CPR on the Dead?

I was a Homicide Sergeant for over two years. During that time, I supervised more than one-hundred murders, stabbings, shootings, beatings and more. After attending several homicide investigative schools and working with other seasoned homicide detectives you learn a lot on how people die, evidence collection and something extremely important, 'Don't let patrol officers in your scene.' They always contaminate the crime scene or screw it up somehow.

I was dispatched to a suspicious death of an elderly female. The victim, Maria, was in her late 60's and lived alone. Maria and her neighbor met every morning and drank Cuban coffee and talked about Cuba and the good life. The neighbor found it unusual that her friend didn't call her on this morning. She knocked on Maria's front door but got no answer. Concerned, she called the police.

This is called a 'Check on the Welfare,' when someone should be home but doesn't answer the door. Two patrol officers arrived, knocked on the door and, like her neighbor, got no response. They called their sergeant for permission to breach the front door and make entry. The sergeant arrived and they used a sledgehammer to get into the house.

The sergeant did not enter the house but spoke to the neighbors about the victim. Minutes later, the two patrol officers exited the house and told the sergeant the victim was dead in the kitchen. Also, there was a lot of blood around her. The sergeant, based on what the two patrol officers told him, sealed the house and requested a homicide detective to respond. I was not too far from the scene, so I told dispatch that I would handle it. I arrived on the scene in about three minutes.

Upon arrival, I interviewed the two officers who stated, "We broke down the door and found the victim dead in a pool of blood on the kitchen floor. There is a thick pool of blood all around her. We didn't want to contaminate the scene, so we backed out of the house and notified our supervisor of what we found."

My first question was, "Did you call fire rescue?" Both officers nodded their heads saying, no, they didn't call. One of them said, "Sergeant Philbrick, this woman's been dead for a while. There is some wet and dried blood all over the kitchen floor. We would have had to walk in the blood to get to her. I know when someone is dead. She's dead."

At that time, the patrol sergeant walked over and told me that the ME (Medical Examiner) was delayed but en route.

I was not sure if this was going to be a homicide or a natural death so I commended them on scene preservation and entered the residence. There was no forced entry by a burglar or thief and inside the house showed no signs of a struggle or fight. Nothing seemed amiss as I made my way to the kitchen.

When I got in the kitchen, I quickly noticed that the pool of blood on the linoleum floor was not that old. It was still wet even though she had been on the floor forat least two hours or more. I didn't see any weapons, bloody kitchen knives, or shell casings. It looks like a natural death.

By now, the neighbor had called the victim's son and daughter. They arrived with four grandchildren and attempted to penetrate the crime scene perimeter but were stopped by uniformed patrol officers.

The neighbor told the family that Maria was dead. The family started crying and screaming. If I remember correctly, fire rescue was called to treat her thirty-five year old daughter. When she heard her mother was dead, she collapsed and was treated fire rescue.

Inside the house, I was searching for clues on how and why she died. The interior of the house provided no clues. I looked at her body and there was no discoloration or pooling of blood in her arms, legs or torso. I found this to be a bit unusual on a dead body that was more than an hour old. I carefully stepped around the pool of blood and touched her body. She was not cold to the touch. If she was dead, her body temperature should have dropped significantly. It hadn't. But she could have died minutes ago.

I then put two fingers on her carotid artery to feel for a pulse. I pressed hard against her throat and thought I felt a pulse, but I wasn't sure. I then opened one of her eyes and her pupil dilated. This was an indication of a live person.

This woman was still alive. What the hell do we do now? The family has been told she was dead and the medical examiner is arriving soon. I thought for a few seconds and went outside.

I walked out the front door and summoned one of the officers to come over to where I was standing. I was in a hurry but wanted to cover one thing. Officer Rodriguez walked over and said, "Yes, Sarge, what can I do for you?"

I asked him, "Did either of you feel for a pulse?"

He replied, "Sergeant, she was dead a long time ago."

So confirmed with him, no one felt the body for warmth or a pulse. He said, "no."

I then replied, "No, she is not dead, she is still alive." I'm thinking how in the hell do I make this right. I got it!

I said to Rodriguez, "First, call fire rescue. Second, go tell the family I started CPR and got a pulse and she's breathing. Tell them I have a faint pulse and she is alive. Go tell the family and get fire rescue here now!" I went back inside to continue CPR and waited for fire rescue. I really didn't do CPR, I waited. She is alive and breathing.

Fire rescue arrived minutes later.

Maria survived the traumatic medical condition. She is alive today. Maria had an aneurysm. This is where the blood vessel walls are weak and rupture. The victim then bleeds a lot and sometimes dies.

Lesson Learned:

In police work, never assume anything. Remember assume makes an ASS out of U and Me. I hope none of her family members read this book.

8.83 Work Release

As the sergeant in Police Training, we were always shorthanded and could use more help. If it wasn't general cleaning of the offices, it was maintenance in the firearms range, storage or the gym. We could always use another person.

Miami-Dade County came up with the genius idea of having criminals who were short timers work at police departments. Most of the inmates were incarcerated for non-violent crimes and were sentenced to less than three years.

The county thought, why not have them work at police departments doing general labor? They would not try to escape because they were getting out in less than four to six months. After working at the police department all day, a corrections van would pick them up and take them back to jail. I personally didn't like the idea because we spent most of our time babysitting the criminals who were there on the work release program.

On this particular day, I needed Robert King, an inmate from the program to help me in the firearms range. The last few times he worked at police training, he asked me if his wife could bring him lunch. I said, "Not a problem, as long as I could look in the lunch bag before she gives it to him." Things were good for a few weeks until….

I couldn't find Robert King in the building, so I went out into the lobby that was enclosed in glass and I saw Robert's girlfriend's car parked on the north side of the parking lot. He was standing next to the driver's door facing the training building with his hands on top of the roof. She was sitting in the driver's seat.

He was on the other side of the car. I'm thinking, were they smoking a cigarette or marijuana, doing drugs, arguing or were they just talking? I couldn't quite see what she was doing, so I got a pair of binoculars from my office and zoomed in on the vehicle and Robert.

After I focused the lenses, I could see exactly what Robert and his girlfriend were doing. She was sitting in the driver's seat and Robert was standing very close to her door. He had his pants halfway down and his girlfriend was giving him 'Head-oral sex.' It was two-twenty in the afternoon and my work release inmate was getting a blow job in front of the police training building. That was the last day we had work release inmates working at the police department.

8.84 Traffic Homicide

It was late one night and I was riding with Officer Jim Poole. Jim was also on the SWAT Team and a good friend of mine.

A commercial van that cleans pools runs a red light and Jim says, "Let's stop this guy and check him out." My reply was, "Jim, I want to go eat. Who gives a shit the guy ran the light?" Jim asked me again, "I want to check him out." I said, "Jim, do what you want but make it snappy, I'm hungry." He activated the blue lights.

The van pulled over to the side of the road. Jim got out and approached the driver. I got out and stood in front of our police car. I was bored and hungry and believed Jim was wasting his time and mine.

Officer Poole walked the driver back to where I was and told me, "I'm going to search his car. I also ran him, and I'm waiting on a reply from dispatch." I talked to the driver about the pool business. His name was Roger Franklin.

Less than a minute later, dispatch raised me, "705" (That was my unit number) and said, "Can you clear from the subject?" Poole was back with me and took a few steps away from the driver. Dispatched asked, "Is the subject in custody?" Poole replied, "We have the subject, but he is not in custody." Dispatch stated, "He is wanted in Minnesota for a homicide." I pulled out my Glock pistol and covered Jim as he handcuffed the subject.

Handcuffed, Roger Franklin looked at me and said, "Well, I guess she died." I asked, "How is that?" Roger said, "I pushed the bitch out of my car. I must have been doing 60-70 miles an hour." I asked, "Who did you push out of the car?" Roger said, "My girlfriend. I was tired of that bitch. It was kind of funny. She held on to the door for a few minutes and I dragged her until she let go."

Later, we learned that she lived for a few hours but died in surgery. She lived long enough to tell the Minnesota State Police who killed her.

Traffic Homicide: Tactical Point

Never assume that anyone is not a threat. I was more concerned with going to eat, than arresting a subject for homicide. That was my error, and it would not happen again.

8.85 Retired on Duty

I really enjoyed my police career. I looked forward to going to work most days. But, after twenty-two years, I knew I wanted to do something different. Here is my last, on-duty police story.

Sergeant Sandy Flutie and I just left the station and were en-route to the Ranch House restaurant for lunch. We were in a surveillance vehicle which was an old beat-up Ford. The vehicle was fast but looked like crap. No one took us for cops unless they were doing something illegal.

I was driving. I stopped for a red light at the intersection of West 12th Avenue and 84th Street. After a few seconds, a brand-new navy blue Camaro pulled up next to us. This car just came off the show room. I'm sure it didn't have more than 500 miles on it.

The Camaro was occupied by two black males, they were not more than twenty years old. They were in a car they couldn't afford. The passenger looked over at me and immediately reached over and touched the driver's arm and said something. He made us.

We call this 'Fish Eyes.' Both males were facing forward, but both of their eyes were concentrated on us. I knew something was wrong. I couldn't get behind them to run the tag, but I could just barely see in the vehicle.

That is when I noticed a blue towel covering the steering column and ignition. The car was stolen. They put a towel over the console to conceal the damage they did to get to the ignition wires. The towel was covering most of the steering column, but I could see there were no keys in the ignition.

Without turning my head toward Flutie, I said, "Sandy, that Camaro to my left is a '22.' What do you think?" A '22' is the police code for a stolen vehicle. Sandy looked over toward the vehicle and said, "Sure is."

From experience, this would have been the next scenario. Sandy and I would back off and get behind the Camaro and run the tag. The car would come back stolen. We would then request a marked unit to stop the car. After a few minutes, the marked unit would arrive and would try to stop the stolen Camaro. That was not going to happen. These guys all run.

The Camaro would attempt to evade the police, and after speeds of 90 to 100 miles an hour, would be involved in a terrific accident after endangering the lives of the public and five or six officers in the high-speed chase. Sandy and I would have initiated the chase and would end up doing 90% of the paperwork. Was it worth it?

I asked Sandy, "What do you want think?"

Flutie nodding his head, replied, "I think the Camaro is most likely stolen."

I then said, "What do you want to do?"

Sandy replied, "I want to go eat. I'm hungry."

I thought for a moment and said, "OK, let's go eat."

I retired three months later.

Chapter Nine

Off Duty

9.01 Robbery at Gunpoint

I own a building on North Dixie Highway and Taft Street in Hollywood. The area is bad but is changing for the better every year. Corporate giants are buying old buildings, fixing them up and moving in. The area has improved since I purchased the 4000 square foot building three years ago.

On the night of the robbery, my wife and I went home early. Something I never do. I don't think the robbery subject knew that. My wife's brother, Raul and her mother Mose were packing my wife's Lexus. Raul was flying back to Suriname the next day. It wasn't too late to be out front, but late enough. Raul was putting his luggage in the car and his mother was going in and out of the business, helping him.

Raul is a businessman in Suriname and purchased car parts and other merchandise he could sell in Suriname. They had just started putting items in the car when a black, Latin male appeared out of nowhere.

He was close to Raul and his mother, Mose. In a milli-second, he drew a Glock firearm from his jacket and pointed the gun at Mose's head. He was about two feet away from her. He yelled at Mose and Raul, "Give me your money and any jewelry you have."

Neither Mose nor Raul wear jewelry, so Raul pulled his pockets our and a few dollars fell to the ground. The robbery subject told them to 'Back up" as he picked up the $18 or 19 dollars. It was not enough.

He then ordered Raul to give him the keys to my wife's 2012 Lexus. Raul dug in his pocket and handed the robbery subject the keys. He then ordered both of them to get down on the cement floor. Reluctantly, Mose and Raul got down on the ground, face down. Raul later told me he thought the gunman was going to kill both of them. He stood there and hesitated on what to do. He still had the Glock pistol in his right hand. Raul stated, "After three to four seconds, which felt like five minutes, the black male pointed the gun at his mother's head and hesitated."

Suddenly he turned and got into the 2012 Lexus. The robbery subject started the Lexus and drove away. Raul called the police and then called me at home.

For safety purposes we have made a few changes.

- Installation of video cameras
- More lighting is better and safer than the old poor lighting. (I have put in new lighting and security cameras that makes the parking lot five times brighter than before.)
- Larger identification numbers on the building so the police can locate us faster.
- Now, no one goes outside alone at night. We travel in pairs. Any female is escorted outside by a capable male.

9.02 Newspaper Route

During my first years of college, I worked for the Miami Herald as a newspaper distributor and area manager. The job started at 4:30 am every day.

I was in school, training in judo, and working every morning delivering newspapers in the Hollywood, Florida area. I had competed in a judo tournament the day before and injured my right arm and shoulder. I had great difficulty moving my right arm and shoulder.

It was about 5:30 am and I was eastbound on Johnson Street in Hollywood. I had just crossed over a small bridge and my car was full of newspapers. Suddenly, right there in front of me, in the middle of the street, were two men. One of the men appeared to be injured. His entire right leg was bandaged, and the other male was holding him up. I slowed and stopped. They came around to the driver's door and said, "My buddy just got out of the hospital. Can you take us to Johnson and US 1?" Reluctantly, I agreed.

Where they wanted to go was just about a mile and a half east of where I was. They both got into my station wagon. I moved the newspapers to the rear of the car.

We didn't speak much driving to US 1 and Johnson Street. I found that a little interesting. When we got to US 1, I pulled over and said, "Here we are. Have a good day." The passenger looked at me and said, "Take us north to the airport." I said, "I have to get these newspapers out and don't have time, please get out." He replied, "I'm not getting out unless you take me and my partner to the airport." The rear guy got out and walked to the passenger front seat and said to his buddy, "Let's go."

Now, I was getting mad. I drove these two guys to where they wanted to go, and now the guy was refusing to leave so I couldn't get back to work.

I got out of the car and walked around to the passenger's door. I opened the door and told the guy to get out. When I said that, he slid over to the driver's seat, put the car in drive and punched the gas. I had left the car running. As he drove off, the open car door threw me backwards onto the ground. I got up and I was pissed! I grabbed the other guy and told him, "Get your friend back here with my car, now!" The guy stealing my car drove around the block, pulled up, opened the passenger door and yelled to his buddy, "Get in!"

The guy standing next to me on the curb had the injured leg. I quickly threw him with a judo throw to the ground and dove into the open door while the driver took off. I was punching him in the face while at the same time trying to turn the car off. After about 150 feet, I finally got the key turned off and out of the ignition. The car abruptly came to a screeching halt.

He jumped out as I was lying there on the seat. My judo injury was killing me. I looked up and both males were running away. I had successfully thwarted an attempt to steal my car. There weren't cell phones back then, so I just finished distributing the newspapers and went home.

I wasn't a police officer back then but luckily, I kept them from stealing my car.

Newspaper Route: Lesson Learned

Don't stop and assist anyone at 4:30 am in the morning. If they block the road like these two guys did, just drive around them.

9.03 Midnight Auto Burglary

I had taken two weeks off work to study for the upcoming sergeant's promotional examination. I was home studying day and night.

It was just past 2:00 am when I heard a vehicle pull up across the street. The muffler was a little loud but that is not what aroused my suspicion. Across the street, was a Masonic Lodge and a parking lot. It was unusual for someone to park there, especially at this hour. The vehicle parking was not what made me suspicious. The two occupants didn't get out of the car for several minutes but when they did, I heard both of them close the vehicle's doors very slowly and quietly. I then got up and looked out the window.

Two white males in their twenties were sneaking up to a Ford Mustang parked in front of a house on 24th Avenue. The taller of the two males used a Slim Jim to disengage the locks as the car door opened. Both males got into the car.

I knew then that I was witnessing a crime in progress. It was either an auto theft or something in the vehicle that they wanted. I went to my bedroom and got my Glock pistol and picked up the phone to call 911 to report a crime in progress. It was too late. Both men were just getting out of the Mustang. One was holding a car radio and the other one had removed several of the air bags from the interior of the car. An airbag has a street value of over one-hundred dollars.

I grabbed my flashlight and slowly walked across the street. When they got into their vehicle, I turned on my flashlight so they couldn't see me and yelled, "Police Officer, you're under arrest!" Once I had them off balance, controlled and leaning on the hood of their car, I called 911 for help.

"This is Officer Philbrick. I am an off-duty police officer and have two subjects at gun point who burglarized a vehicle at 406 N. 24th Avenue. I need an officer here now."

In less than a minute, you could hear the police units coming. It was now about two-twenty-five in the morning, and it felt good to know that I wasn't alone out here as the units started to arrive.

When they came, I had my badge in my hand and showed it to each officer until I was told, "We got this." Both subjects were arrested and charged with grand theft and burglary.

Midnight Auto Burglary: Training Point

The point of the story is that it doesn't matter if you are a police officer or a civilian. If you decide to take action, you have to have a plan, react quickly and get the police there as soon as possible. It is extremely dangerous for anyone, even a police officer, to detain two criminals by yourself for any length of time.

If you decide to take action, be firm, authoritative and decisive. Help will arrive, but you must control the situation for at least two to three minutes until help or backup gets there. The best and safest thing to do is call the police and give them as much information as you can. Stay on the line until the police arrive or you are told to hang up the phone.

9.04 Become the Tiger

One night, I was washing my car in front of my business. It was about 11:30 pm. My business is in between two buildings with the glass doors located in the rear. You wouldn't see the office front doors or me unless you were looking for it. I was washing my car about 45-50 feet away from the main road. It was dark out but the streetlights illuminated the driveway just enough for me to wash my car.

A few minutes earlier, I had noticed a tall, white male walking eastbound on Hollywood Boulevard. He was across the street and walking away from me. He was about 6' tall and appeared to weigh over 200 pounds. I took a quick look at him but up to now, he hadn't done anything. I just took note of him as being a little bit unusual.

However, a few minutes had passed, and he was now standing at the edge of my driveway, looking at me. He paused briefly, looked around and then started walking toward me. He was now about 30 feet from me and walking directly to where I was standing.

I usually kept a gun in my car at all times, but because I was washing my car, I had put it in my glove box. As the man kept walking toward me, I knew I had a potential problem. He looked suspicious and a 'little nuts.' I didn't know him, and he was coming toward me with a purpose. Worst of all, I couldn't see his hands.

Without taking my eyes off the man, I reached into my car and picked up the first thing I could find to use as a weapon. Unfortunately, it was my black plastic hairbrush. I hid it behind my back as if it were a gun or a weapon. I then opened the car door and tried to use it for a safety barrier if he decided to attack me. He was now coming toward me at a faster pace than a normal walk. He was now about 15 feet away. So far, we were about 5-6 seconds into this event.

The subject observed me reach inside my car and was now coming at me faster. He was not running, but his pace had quickened. He had no idea what I picked up from the car but he did have a look of concern on his face as he closed in on me. I was behind the open door of my Honda. I was trying to shield myself in the event he had a weapon or attacked me.

He was now about 10 feet away. I looked at him and yelled as loud as I could, "Stop right there. Take one more step and I will fucking kill you." I showed him the object in my hand. He immediately stopped. He probably thought I had a gun in my hand. He couldn't tell it was just my hairbrush. I had grabbed the hairbrush by the brush needles, and the black handle resembled the barrel of a gun in the darkness. The man paused for a few seconds, barked several obscenities at me and turned and walked away.

Was I rude to this individual? Absolutely, yes! But, honestly, I didn't care if I was rude or hurt his feelings. What were his intentions; to help me? A stranger was going to help me wash my car in the middle of the night? I don't think so. He may have had a gun or weapon, and most likely was going to rob me. He never said a word to me until he stopped and decided not to attack me.

He stalked me for a few minutes and thought that I would be an easy victim. But I wasn't an easy target. I took control of the situation and became the aggressor, not the victim. I became the tiger and not the lamb that he expected.

Become the Tiger: Teaching Point

If you are confronted and threatened by an attacker, they will expect you to cower and become the victim. They will choose what they think is an easy mark. But, if you become the tiger before the attack escalates, it will cut your chances of being a victim by more than fifty percent.

The decision to resist depends on what he wants. If he decides to take your wife with him, it's time to become the tiger. I he just wants money and your watch, give it to him. Nothing you own is worth dying for.

9.05 Gun Shots at Home

One Saturday morning around 3:00 am, my girlfriend and I were in bed sleeping. We lived together in my home in east Hollywood, Florida. Suddenly, I was awakened by the sound of glass breaking in the kitchen and living room. I sat up in bed and heard the sounds of three bullets ricocheting off the walls and that distinct sound a bullet makes as it whizzes through the air. Somebody was shooting into my house.

I got out of bed and grabbed my gun that was on the night stand. I heard pop, pop, and then pop again. I could now see three more bullets penetrating the dry wall in my kitchen and living room. There was fine dust in the air from the bullets entering the dry wall and exiting. At the same time I could hear the china dishes in my kitchen breaking. I yelled to Shawnee, "Call the police and get down, someone is shooting at us." Then I heard a car speeding away from the front of my house.

I ran outside holding my Glock pistol. The car was gone. I looked down and noticed I was naked not wearing a stitch of clothing and immediately ran back into the house. Someone had just fired six bullets into my house through the front door and windows.

Minutes later, the Hollywood Police arrived. There were no shell casings in my yard or on the street where the shots came from. It was obvious that the shooter used a six shot revolver.

I believed this was more of a message than someone trying to kill me. I got the message, but I didn't stop being a proactive police officer.

I thought I could fly above the radar and continue to put people in jail, and I would be forgotten by those individuals who lost thousands of dollars in cash and a couple hundred kilos of cocaine. Boy, was I wrong!

They might be in jail, but they could easily order a hit on me from prison. When I put the Seminola gang in jail, DEA, ATF, FBI and Customs impounded their vehicles, took their homes and life savings. I could understand why they would be pissed. Maybe revenge was in the cards.

Since that night, I kept a much lower personal profile, changed public listings of my address to the police station, and took my name, phone number and address out of the phone book. I've been pretty safe since doing that.

Gunshots at Home: Learning Point

How does this apply to you? I want you to fly under the radar. Why? For the safety of your kids and your family. You can do this by not displaying wealth when you have it. If people know you have money, they will target you. Do not be unnecessarily flashy. You will read further in the book where a home owner purchased a new car and they became the victim of a home invasion robbery. During the robbery one of the robber's stated, "You can afford a new Road Ranger then you must have a lot of cash."

When you get that big commission check on your latest deal, keep it to yourself and your family. It is nobody else's business. Don't flaunt what you have. Enjoy it, but be responsible. Keep a low profile. That way, thieves will not try to take it from you. If they don't know you have it, you and your family will not become targets.

But, as a police officer, who put them in jail, I have one thing to say, "Bring it on, I will be ready next time!"

9.06 Getting Cut on Video

Not long ago, a news crew flew in from France to videotape my counter-terrorism class. I was teaching classes on how to defend yourself on a commercial aircraft if a terrorist had knives and was hijacking the plane. They wanted me to show the technique of taking off my shoes and putting them on my hands and then defending myself against a knife attack.

During one of the demonstrations, I decided to use a real buck knife for the video news crew. I wanted it to look as real as possible rather than use a rubber knife. It was going to be in slow motion. The reporter was to attack me, step by step, in slow motion so the camera crew could videotape the knife attack sequence and then my defense. We discussed and rehearsed it three times.

Camera's rolling. The female reporter came at me with the very sharp double-edged buck knife. I reacted as planned but she didn't follow the script. I went up and she went down, cutting my right thumb wide open with the knife. She had cut my thumb deep with the knife. Knowing we were taking video I continued the technique and defended myself and then took the knife away from her. The blood from the laceration on my thumb was going everywhere.

After the cameras were off I re-enactment and demonstrated just how easy it is to get cut during a knife fight, or even a simple demonstration.

Getting Cut on Video: Teaching Point

If you decide to defend against a knife attack, you will get cut. Minimize your injuries.

9.07 The Subway Robbery

I had just finished working out and was driving home from the police department. I always worked out in the gym at the end of my shift. I was dressed in sweatpants and a gym shirt. I stopped off at the Subway on Young Circle to take home a tuna sub. I always eat, watch TV and relax before I go to bed. It was just before midnight.

I usually carry a gun with me, but this time, I left it in the car. I didn't carry it because I didn't want my sweat to ruin the finish on the Smith & Wesson 2-inch revolver. I was wet and sweaty from working out. I entered the Subway just before they closed. It was exactly 11:48 pm.

I ordered my sandwich and the guy behind the counter made the sub and rolled it in the wax paper and put it on the counter. When he did that, I heard the glass door open behind me. The Subway employee looked at the two guys who had just walked in. I watched his eyes get huge. He looked at them again and then looked at me. He knew I was a police officer. I turned and looked over my left shoulder.

Standing inside the door, were two Latin males, both in their mid to late 20's. They were both wearing long, gray raincoats and it wasn't raining outside. In fact, it was hot and humid. Both of the subjects had something in their hands under their raincoats. I thought I saw the barrel of a shotgun. Now, like clockwork they both rotated. They were now standing with their backs to each other. One subject was facing the counter and the other was facing out of the glass door.

The time lapse as all this occurred was about five seconds. I realized I was standing in the middle of a robbery and I was going to be one of the victims. Also, at that moment, I was wearing a very expensive Rolex watch and had no gun on me. Good job, Mr. Policeman, you are about to get robbed and have no gun.

I was actually holding the 12-inch sub. I put it down and in less than a second, I moved down the counter and stood in front of the Latin male facing the counter. I was about two feet from him, and I took a fighting position and brought both hands up to a boxer's position. I looked him right in the eye and yelled, "Come on, do it! Let's do it!" As I was yelling at him, I was slapping my hands together right in front of his face. This all took about three seconds.

My plan was when the male in front of me raised the shotgun from the raincoat, I was going to grab it, hit him in the face with it while he was still holding it and then take the gun away.

As I backed up along the counter, I saw myself shooting both subjects at the door. I was really not sure if I could pull it off, but it sounded like a pretty good plan at the time.

The time lapse in this robbery was now about 10-12 seconds. In that time, I had prepared myself for battle, formulated a plan, made a decision to attack, and quickly moved down the counter and confronted the armed robbery subjects. Looking back, it really wasn't too smart.

Now, back to the robbery. I was in a fighting stance, clapping my hands, yelling at the top of my lungs and the guy in front of me said to his partner, without ever turning around, "Let's get out of here." With that, he rotated like a soldier and they both fled out of the store and ran around the building.

I quickly turned to the cashier as he yelled, "Oh my God, those guys were going to rob us. They have been here three times tonight." I yelled back, "Call the police now!"

I went out to my car and got my gun and stayed with the cashier until the police arrived.

They never did catch the two robbery subjects. Looking back, I sometimes ask myself, did I make the right decision? The answer is 'Yes.' I survived this time and wasn't the laughingstock of my police department.

One good thing, the cashier didn't charge me for my tuna sub. I had risked my life for a $7.00 tuna sub.

The Subway Robbery: Survival Point

Remember the principles of surviving. When I realized I was in danger, I immediately obtained a tactical mental mindset. I then formulated a plan and surprised the robbery subjects by taking the fight to them. I had the skills, but not the equipment to carry out the defense. I took the offensive and attacked. With my training and martial arts skill level, I felt as though

I could resist and survive the attack. Bottom line, I prevented an armed robbery.

I am not advocating or recommending you try and prevent an armed robbery. I just acted on instinct and surprised the two subjects. They didn't plan on someone preventing their robbery. If you own a gun, carry it!

9.08 Smoking Kills

This is a story about a police sniper that had been given the green light to kill a man who was shooting at the police from his condominium on the 15th floor. The police sniper was waiting for the window of opportunity. If you are patient, it will come.

I first met Jim Cruz, the shooter, when I opened my gun store in downtown Hollywood. He was a Viet Nam Vet, a gun guy and a take charge person. I hired his wife Marie to do my books and Jim helped me in the gun store for a short period of time. I liked Jim, but he was a little wacky and had a very aggressive personality. I also thought he drank a lot but I never saw him intoxicated. At the store, he would do what he thought was right and not what I wanted. It was an issue that was coming to an end.

After a few months, I fired him and his wife. I told him, "Jim, I can't fire you and not fire your wife also." He reluctantly understood and I was happy he was gone. I just knew I had to separate myself from him. I didn't know why, or what it was, but I just had that gut feeling that one day he would be a problem.

We still remained friends and would have coffee once in a while. I had dinner one night at his condo on the beach in Hollywood. He was 15 floors up and had a nice little two-bedroom apartment facing south with an ocean and Ocean Drive view.

One night, Jim and Marie got into a domestic argument and she called the Hollywood Police. As the two patrol officers arrived, and were about to exit the elevator, Jim greeted the two uniformed men with a burst of gun fire from his AR-15 assault rifle. Both officers escaped injury and called for help.

Jim fired eight rounds into the elevator. The Hollywood Police SWAT Team was called out. My good friend, Sgt. Ward Stanley was the team leader. As more police officers were arriving, Jim started shooting from his 15th story condominium balcony.

By the time the SWAT Team arrived, Jim had shot up four or five marked police cars and fired over 100 rounds from his AR-15 assault rifle. Marie, his wife, escaped down the stairs when he fired at the uniformed officers. She told Sgt. Stanley that her husband was drunk.

The Sergeant placed a counter sniper team in the condominium just south of Jim's apartment. The sniper and spotter were positioned on the 17th floor of the condominium. They were two floors up. They had a good advantage view of Jim and his apartment.

It was dark now and Jim had barricaded his front door with furniture and was shooting from behind his couch on the balcony. He was tearing up police vehicles with his high powered .223 assault rifle. So far, no police officers had been injured.

Jim continued shooting at the police for the next twenty minutes. The sniper was given the 'green light' on Jim. He was still drinking, smoking and shooting. It's funny now, but those were the three things he most liked to do.

Sgt. Stanley called me from the scene to tell me, "Guess what your friend is doing?" Heck, I didn't know, and I said, "What is he doing?" Stanley replied, "He's barricaded in his condo shooting out of his balcony." When Sgt. Stanley told me what Jim was doing, I thought for a moment, should I go there and try to talk him down? Before I could say anything, Stanley said, "I have to go" and hung up the phone.

Two hours later, Sgt. Stanley called me and told me that just after 8.45pm the sniper took his shot and killed Jim. Snipers have a credo. It is 'One Shot, One Kill."

A week later, the sniper who killed Jim came by my office. Being in SWAT in Hialeah, I knew the sniper quite well and I asked him to tell me what happened. Richard said, "Wally, your buddy, Jim had turned off all the lights in his apartment. I couldn't see him. I had a good position two floors above his condo but still waited for the shot. I couldn't see shit. Your buddy was pretty tactical for a while, but he was drinking pretty heavily.

Richard continued, "It was pitch dark when I took the shot that killed him. All I could see was him putting a cigarette in his mouth and lighting it with his lighter. He took one puff on the cigarette and that is when I measured down ten inches from the cigarettes glow and fired one round. I couldn't see him when I shot him. I thought I missed because he jumped behind the couch. Minutes later, the SWAT Team made entry into the apartment and found Jim dead behind the couch. He didn't jump. The bullet's impact threw him behind the couch. Jim was shot with a 308 round, which is a pretty good size bullet. He was wearing a ballistic vest but it would not stop a rifle round of that velocity."

At the end of the night, Jim had fired 118 rounds from his AR-15 assault rifle. No police officers were injured or shot.

At the funeral, his wife Marie told me, "If Jim wanted to kill a police officer he would have done it. He was too good of a shot to miss more than one-hundred times." Marie gave me Jim's buck knife he carried in Viet Nam.

Smoking Kills: Tactical Point

The point of the story is the sniper waited and waited for that one moment of opportunity. When Jim took that puff on his cigarette, the flow gave the sniper his target. He measured down to where his chest was and fired one shot.

Sorry Jim, but smoking does kill.

9.09 PBA Fishing Tournament

A lot of police officers like to fish for relaxation. On this day, the Police Benevolent Association was hosting a fishing tournament in Sunny Isles. More than forty boats loaded with off duty police officers paid an entry fee that went to charity. Whichever boat caught the most fish would win.

In the Hialeah boat, were Sandy Flutie, Jeff Shaw, Bob Polink and Tommy Hopkins. All of them were police officers in Hialeah. They left the dock and headed out to sea to find a good deep-water fishing spot.

When they were about two miles out, Sandy saw something floating in the water about one hundred yards from the boat. They drove the eighteen-foot Whaler to the object to see what it was.

At first, they thought it might be a body, a submerged boat or a large dead fish. It wasn't any one of those things. The closer they got, the more they became interested in the floating object. It was square and wrapped in a protective waterproof cover. Then Sandy yelled out, "Holy shit, it's a bale of marijuana." It was a 150-pound bale of marijuana floating in the ocean.

Bob and Jeff got a hook and gigged the huge bale and pulled it into the boat. Then Hopkins said, "There's another one." After recovering the second bale of marijuana they spotted several more. They hauled in six bales of marijuana and called the US Coast Guard.

Later, they were told that early in the morning, a 'go fast boat' was detected by radar and chased by US Customs and the Coast Guard. When they finally boarded the boat after a twenty-minute chase, the boat was clean. They had already met another boat and unloaded the marijuana or thrown it overboard into the ocean. I guess we know now where the marijuana went.

When the Coast Guard arrived and saw the bales piled up in Jeff's 18' Whaler, they thought that Jeff's boat was the pick-up boat. During the high-speed chase, the drug traffickers threw three thousand pounds of marijuana into the ocean last night. Initially, the Fed's treated the four Hialeah police officers as co-conspirators of the marijuana drop.

After an hour of interviews and background checks, the US Coast Guard and US Customs finally believed the four cops. They didn't catch any fish that day but recovered hundreds of thousands of dollars of marijuana. You never know what you're going to catch in the Atlantic.

9.10 The Stripper and the Terrorist

In July, 2001, two months before 911, I met two of the 18 terrorist hijackers that flew a 757 jet into the World Trade Center. They came to my business, the '911 Store' where I had a gun shop and a private investigations business. Two of them wanted a background investigation to find someone.

The two terrorists were Waleed Al-Shehri and his brother, Wail Al-Shehri, who later hijacked American Airlines Flight 11 on route to Los Angeles from Boston and flew the plane into the World Trade Center.

It is a well-documented fact that the 911 terrorists were not your typical Muslim terrorists. They frequented adult clubs where all the female dancers performed naked. These terrorists like lap dances and the champagne room where you could pay for sex and get whatever you wanted. They also hired prostitutes and rented pornographic videos. They had plenty of money and time.

In 2001, I was working as a licensed private investigator and could locate people and conduct background checks. In July of 2001, I received a phone call from a woman. It was almost 8pm on a Monday night and I was trying to go home. She called the investigative line and wanted to meet with me now. I said, "Miss, it's almost 8 o'clock. Can it wait until tomorrow?" She replied, "No, I work tonight at 10pm. I'm an exotic dancer and this guy is stalking me." When I heard she was a nude dancer, I decided to stay. She arrived about fifteen minutes later.

I can't give you her name, but let's call her Susan Adams. She was very attractive and had the body that most women would kill for. Now you know why she danced nude.

She told me she met this Saudi Arabian guy at the club she danced at. They were together for several months and she decided to end the relationship. Susan told me that this guy was stalking her, and she was afraid of him. She then told me she may be pregnant with this man's child. She wanted to hire me so this guy couldn't find her even if he went to another private investigator. She wanted to leave South Florida and did not want to go to any place where he could find her.

What she wanted was a dossier. A dossier would give the recipient all of their relatives, places you once lived, friends, family members and neighbors. It's great for skip tracing. All I had to do was run a comprehensive dossier on her and I would get her life history. I asked her what her date of birth was and social security number. I then went into my investigative data base and ran a complete dossier on her. I charged her $100.

I asked her who was stalking her, and she told me his name was Waleed Al- Shehri.

She told me that he was not working but was in school as a student. He was learning to fly planes. He had a lot of money. She was afraid that he would find her and possibly hurt her. She wanted to know where she could go to be safe from this guy. Susan said he was jealous and extremely possessive. I ran the dossier on the client, Susan Adams.

When the printout was completed, I sat down with her and showed her places she should not go. He would be able to find her at those addresses if he did what she was doing now and went to a private investigator. She was amazed at all of the addresses of relatives, family and friends that were listed on the report. I told her she could be safe if she did not go to any of the addresses listed in the dossier. She thanked me and left around 8.15 that night.

The next day:

It was Tuesday morning and I had just gotten back from breakfast. I was paged to come to the front of the '911 Store.' Someone was in the store and wanted an investigation completed. I went out front and I was greeted by two Middle Eastern men. This was the first time I'd met the two clients. They were Waleed Al-Shehri and his brother Wail Al-Shehri. I asked them how I could help them and Waleed Stated. "I want to locate someone." I said, "Fine, let's go back to my office."

We sat down in my conference room, and after formal greetings, I asked them, "Who do you need help in locating?" Waleed told me he wanted to find his girlfriend. She may be pregnant, and she left him. I asked him, "What is her name?" He replied "Susan Adams." I almost fell off my chair.

What are the chances of two distinct parties coming to the same investigative office one day apart? One client wanted to hide from the other party and the other party wanted me to locate the client that was hiding from him. I first thought it was set up from the State but soon disregarded that. Since 2001, the laws have changed on locating people. Today, I would not be able to give him the information due to stricter laws on the release of private information.

I told Waleed Al-Shehri nothing. I took the information on Susan Adams and told him to call me the next day. He paid me $100 cash. He and his brother left. I still had a copy of the report from last night on Susan Adams. If I gave him the report and information, it would certainly be unethical as a private investigator and certainly a conflict of interest. If I did not do the background, Al-Shehri would just go to another investigator. I decided to send him to another agency with an investigator I knew well.

I called Francois, the other investigator, and told him I was going to send him a client who wanted a background check to locate someone. I told him what to collect from the client and actually gave him a copy of the report I ran for Susan Adams.

I met with Waleed Al-Shehri and Wail Al-Shehri the next day. I told him if I conducted a background to locate his girlfriend it would be a conflict of interest. He asked me, "Why would it be a conflict of interest?" I told him it was confidential, and I could not tell him. He was not happy. I refunded him his $100.

I didn't know at that time he was a terrorist, so I treated him like an investigative client. I then told him that a friend of mine who was a private investigator would run the background check for him and give him the exact same results that I would. He seemed content. I gave him Francois's phone number. He called Francois that day and got the printout and background information on his girlfriend, Susan Adams.

On September 11, 2001, just a few months after trying to locate his girlfriend, Wail and Waleed Al-Shehri hijacked a Boeing 757 aircraft and both of them died when their American Airlines flight flew into the first World Trade Center tower.

When I heard the names, it still didn't ring a bell until, September 14, 2001. Two FBI agents knocked on my door and asked me my association with Wail Al-Shehri and his brother Waleed Al-Shehri. It was reported that their luggage never made it onto the American Airlines Flight from Boston to Los Angeles. There was not enough room in the aircraft, so the luggage was scheduled to go out on the next flight to LA. After the terrorist attack on the World Trade Center, they searched his luggage and found my business card.

9-11 was the first time terrorists hijacked a commercial airline and flew it into a Federal Building.

9.11   Robbery at the Movies

On this particular night, my girlfriend Shawnee and I were out to dinner and a movie with four of our friends. There were six of us altogether. Pete Lacroix and his wife were both black belts in judo. Charlie Tiger and his girlfriend were both police officers. I was with my girlfriend, Shawnee Fross. She was a police officer in Hollywood, and I was a police officer in Hialeah.

In the group of six, four of us were black belts in judo and four of the six were police officers. Can you imagine that someone decided to rob us?

As we were walking out of the movie theatre, a car drove by and the passenger climbed half way out of the vehicle and grabbed Mary's purse. She was trying to hold on to her purse as she fell to the ground and the strap of the purse broke. Pete yelled out, "They grabbed Mary's purse!" The black Ford then sped out of the movie parking lot southbound on State Road 7.

Shawnee and I started running to our vehicle and Charlie and his girlfriend ran to their car, while Pete and Mary were shocked, standing in the parking lot. The chase was on. We were all in civilian clothes and in our personal vehicles.

Shawnee and I argued over who was going to drive because she had jurisdiction. The strong-armed robbery occurred in Hollywood. I told her I would drive while she got on the radio and advised dispatch. She agreed. Charlie and I pulled out at the exact same time and drove southbound on State Road 7, looking for the robbery subjects. Pete and Mary were trying to catch up.

After only about a minute, I saw the black Ford Torino at the intersection of Pembroke Road and State Road 7. It was the last car in line at the light. I yelled to Charlie to take the passenger and I would take the driver. We all screeched up in our personal cars and got out with our guns drawn.

Charlie blocked the car in from the rear and I wedged my Honda in between the subject's car and the car in front of him. The driver was a male and the passenger who grabbed the purse was a female.

The four of us got out with guns in our hands. I yelled to the driver, "Police Officers, put your hands in the air and get out of the vehicle!" He opened the door and I grabbed him. I laid him out spread eagle on the pavement in the middle of the intersection. Meanwhile, Charlie and his girlfriend got the passenger out and placed her on the ground also. Not one of us had a pair of handcuffs. We had to wait for a marked unit that arrived in the next minute. Pete and Mary pulled up and helped with traffic control.

We recovered Mary's purse from inside the vehicle and arrested both subjects for strong-armed robbery. Can you imagine the luck of those two robbers? They decided to rob a group of individuals, four of which were police officers and two of which were black belts in judo.

Later, we learned that the same pair of robbery subjects, just last week, committed a strong-armed robbery in Lauderhill. They dragged and elderly female with their vehicle as she held onto her purse. She almost died from her injuries.

Robbery at the Movies: Tactical Lesson

The lesson from this war story is that you can be attacked at any time or anywhere, and the bad guys really don't care who you are. This night, the bad guys picked the wrong victims.

9.12 Trapped at the Gas Pump

I pulled into the gas station to get some gas. As I got out and opened my door, out of nowhere a subject approached me.

He didn't ask me for money; he was telling me he needed money. I didn't like that. I said to him as I closed the door and started moving away from him, "I don't have any extra money tonight, have a good night." I didn't give him a chance to respond. I made sure I was a good distance from him, and I walked inside the store.

After paying for gas and a sandwich, I walked outside and started to pump gas into my car. Now, the homeless man, who again looked dangerous and menacing, walked up to the customer behind my car. There was a female pumping gas into her silver Acura.

This subject was frightening. He was over 6' tall and weighed over 250 pounds. The drunk walked up to her and stood about 2 feet from her and said, "Can you give me some money for food?" She was trapped, while she continued to pump the gas. She put her purse under her arm and looked at me terrified. He eyes and body language said, "Can you help me?"

I looked at him and barked, "Hey buddy, leave the lady alone." His response was, "I'm not talking to you." She looked at me again for help. I really didn't want to fight this guy. I just wanted him to leave her alone so she could pump gas in her car and go home. I took my cell phone out of my top pocket and held it in the air. Then I said, "Hey, if you don't back away from the lady, I'm going to call 911 and give the police your description and tell them what you are doing." He was focused on the female and never looked up at me. Then he snarled, "You're an asshole." That is when I said, "OK, I'm dialing 911 now." All this time, I was pumping gas into my car.

I stopped pumping gas for a minute and simulated dialing the phone. I said on the phone, "I have a problem. I'm at the Shell station on Ocean Drive." Now he's looking at me. He backed away from the lady. That is when I said, "Keep moving pal, the police are on route."

The guy turned and started walking away at a very fast pace in the opposite direction. I kept watching him and finished pumping my gas. By that time, the lady in the Acura had finished pumping her gas, gotten in her car and she was gone. Gee, she could have said "Thanks."

Trapped at the Gas Pumps: Moral Point

Don't be intimidated by someone when you have support from other people. Here, the woman had me, employees in the store and other customers that drove up to help her. Some people will jump in and help if you just ask.

9.13 Burglary I'm the Victim

I was a police officer in South Florida, and I had just bought a house in West Palm Beach. It was a nice-sized home on one acre. I bought it so my seven-year old son would have a place to play.

When I purchased the home, it didn't have a burglar alarm or video surveillance system. I didn't care because it was my second home and I wouldn't keep anything of real value in it. We moved in slowly, buying furniture as I could afford it.

I kept a written daily planner with things I have to do every day. Doing this keeps me organized. When I purchased the home, I wrote in my planner, 'Get an alarm system.' But I kept putting it off. We usually don't react until something happens. Well, as luck would have it, someone broke into my house.

I never had the alarm system installed. I thought I was safe because there was nothing of real value in the home except furniture and a small amount of jewelry. Also, a Broward Deputy lived two houses down the street. I thought I was fairly safe. Wrong!

The day of the burglary, I got a call from my neighbor. He told me that there was a van parked in front of my house. And, there were two men in blue jumpsuits running out of the front door. One of them was carrying a pillowcase. I told him to hang up the phone and call the police. I also hung up and immediately called 911.

I arrived at my house about one and a half hours later. The two burglars tried to pry my front door open with a crowbar and totally destroyed it. They didn't get in that way, but they did cause extensive damage to the door, locks, and door guard. They then decided upon a second point of entry. They broke the front glass window, reached in and unlocked the latch, pushed the sliding glass window up and crawled into the house, entering my dining room.

The burglars ransacked my home and stole my girlfriend's jewelry box, my son's video game system and my new 60" high-definition flat screen TV. Insurance covered part of the loss, but they absolutely destroyed my front door and exterior window, which I had to pay for myself.

Even though I was a police officer, the whole experience threw me. I finally understood how some victims have emotional trauma after these things happen. After the break-in, I felt as though the burglars would come back. I was afraid to go out and get a new television for fear that they might see the empty box from the new TV and come back and steal it. I expected this behavior, but my son didn't.

My son was terrified and traumatized that 'bad guys' had been in his room and had stolen his gaming system. I was angry for a long time afterwards because of the theft, damage to my house and the emotional trauma to my son. But mainly, I was angry with myself for not getting a security system installed when I moved in. Not only that, but the entire experience was especially humiliating because I had been teaching crime prevention classes at the time.

A few months after the burglary, I went in my garage to get my electric drill, only to find the thugs had taken that as well. I'm sure that there were other things that were taken that I still didn't know about. Honestly, at this point, I just wish I would have bought the alarm before and not after the burglary. Listen to a man with experience. If you do not have an alarm system in your home, go buy one today!

Let's try to change the odds and make you and your family less vulnerable. Be prepared for anything!

9.14 Terrorist and the FBI

I owned and operated a gun store and firearms range in Hollywood, Florida for over eighteen years. During that time, I helped the FBI on three separate terrorist investigations. Terrorists visited the '911 Store' frequently because they could buy guns and police equipment.

In this section, you will learn about two of my employees who positively identified two terrorist cells in South Florida. We notified the FBI and they did absolutely nothing. You will read where Michael Berry, an Israeli Mossad agent here in Hollywood followed the terrorist cell for over two weeks. This group flew one of the American Airline 757 jets into the World Trade Center on 9-11.

I gave the FBI the informant's information and they did nothing.

Michael Berry: Israeli Mossad?

I owned and operated a private investigative agency for over twenty years. One of my private investigators was Michael Berry. He was first introduced to me by his two cousins who owned a business and worked here in the Hollywood/Ft. Lauderdale area. Both cousins were Israeli and manufactured high tech security and spy equipment. Together, they manufactured covert cameras, high-tech listening devices, bug detectors, voice analyzers, mini cameras and anything to do with the spy industry.

Michael Berry, most likely was a member of the Mossad or the Israeli Secret Police. While he was in South Florida, he and my armorer, Robert Kennedy, independently conducted surveillance on a terrorist cell in Hollywood, Florida for weeks.

Berry also recorded conversations the terrorists had with each other at the Mosque in Pembroke Pines. At the beginning, he was just suspicious of the group, but after a few weeks, Berry told me he confirmed that they were terrorists and they had an agenda with selected targets. He told me the terrorists were well funded with lots of cash. He also told me they were training in South Florida for a terrorist attack. Berry told me that the planned attacks would be on American soil.

Before I go any further, I must introduce you to another character in this story. His name is Robert Kennedy. He was a former Navy SEAL.

He worked here at the '911 Store' as my firearms instructor and range officer. Kennedy had the nickname of 'Rat.' As a Vietnam veteran, he would search out the Viet Cong by going into their underground tunnels and flush them out.

One of Kennedy's friends was Howard Gilbert. Gilbert had been coming around the gun shop for about six months and professed he was a defensive tactics expert and a firearms and knife instructor. He claimed that he was a former Marine and told us he was a Federal Agent. We never took Howard too seriously. Maybe we should have.

Howard Gilbert, knowing that Michael Berry, being from Israel hated terrorists teamed up with him. He told Berry that he was an undercover FBI informant. Gilbert told Berry about a terrorist organization here in Hollywood.

Howard Gilbert told Michael Berry that he infiltrated a terrorist cell. Berry and Gilbert then teamed up to investigate the terrorist group in Hollywood. Berry went undercover to find out more about the 'terrorists' Gilbert was training. He stated visiting the local Islamic Mosque where the terrorists met. Berry later told me that one night he recorded 140 minutes of conversation between several of the terrorists.

Gilbert also told me the same thing but did not tell me they were terrorists. At that time, I didn't pay much attention to what he was saying, but maybe I should have. Gilbert told me he was training a small group of Middle Eastern men in knife attack sequences and fundamentals.

That should have been a red flag for anyone, including me. They were being trained in offensive techniques and not defensive. This was a danger sign, but even I missed it. It is now a well-documented fact that Howard Gilbert was training 9-11 terrorists at the US 1 Fitness Gym here in Hollywood on US 1.

FBI Informant: Howard Gilbert

Michael Berry told me that he overheard the terrorists talking about a payoff of $30,000 to a marine who was giving them information on target sites. They were most likely referring to Howard Gilbert, who was working for the FBI in an undercover capacity.

Berry also followed one of the terrorists to the Miami Airport, where he met another associate. Berry told me that the FBI had bugged his phones to find out what he knew about the terrorists.

The press and news agencies wrote several stories in the aftermath of 9-11 about the FBI tapping phones and then being ordered to shut down all of the wire taps. When Berry recorded the terrorist's conversation, that was a felony and the FBI told him that. Even though Berry had discovered a terrorist group in South Florida, the FBI did nothing in-regards to investigating the terrorist cell. The FBI knew about the cell.

Howard Gilbert, their informant told them that he was training them in knife techniques. The covert surveillance that Berry conducted confirmed terrorist activity in South Florida. Therefore, this proves the FBI had solid information on the 9-11 terrorists roughly four months before the attacks.

On Monday, May 14, 2001, Michael Berry came to my business and asked to meet with me. He said it was important. I was talking to an associate of mine and I ended that conversation so I could meet with him. What Michael wanted to tell me seemed very important. He told me the following story:

Howard Gilbert told Michael Berry that he was working for the FBI and had infiltrated a terrorist cell. Berry and Gilbert then teamed up with the Navy Seal, Kennedy and together, investigated the terrorist group in Hollywood. Berry went undercover to find out more about the terrorists while Gilbert was still doing the knife training. Kennedy made several clandestine trips to the Mosque.

Michael Berry, Robert Kennedy and Howard Gilbert covertly entered the local Islamic Mosque in Pembroke Pines. This was where the terrorists met. Berry told me that he overheard the terrorists talking about a payoff of $30,000 to a marine who was giving them information on target sites.

Kennedy: The Navy Seal

Robert Kennedy and Howard Gilbert shared a small house together in east Hollywood. After the 9-11 attacks, "Rat" or Robert Kennedy decided to quit working for me at the '911 Store' and leave South Florida for a while. The FBI and news crews were always searching for a story and he didn't want to give them one. He went to Iraq as a contractor. Howard Gilbert stayed in Hollywood.

Before the attacks on the World Trade Center, I spoke to Kennedy and he told me that there was a time when Gilbert was on 'High Alert." He believed that the terrorists were going to go operational and do something bad at Cape Canaveral. Gilbert believed the terrorists were up to no good as well, due to them learning only offensive and not defensive knife techniques. Gilbert told Kennedy that he could not get any of the 'good guys' or the FBI to believe him. Rat told me that Gilbert was teaching the terrorists at the US 1 Fitness Center about two miles from where we were. Once he went with Gilbert to the Mosque at Pembroke Pines. They were acting as if they were 'anti-America.' While at the Mosque, Gilbert introduced Kennedy to the Imam. Rat said, "They did not trust me. I did not see anything that was unusual, but I did have a very bad 'gut feeling' while I was there"

Surveillance of the Terrorists

Michael Berry decided to follow Howard Gilbert and the terrorists, to find out who they were meeting. He told me he followed them to Mosques, covert meetings, Miami International Airport and several other locations. Berry said he followed several terrorists alone for weeks and for hundreds of hours. One night, Berry and Kennedy entered the Mosque in Pembroke Pines after hours and conducted covert surveillance on the members and their activities inside the mosque.

Berry was convinced they were a terrorist cell. He had been monitoring the group for weeks in Hollywood, Miami and the South Florida area. Berry told me, "They have plenty of money and actually have targets, dates and times." I asked him, "Why don't you go to the FBI?" He said, "I did. I first went to the Israeli Embassy, who introduced me to the FBI in the main office. I told them about the terrorists but when I told them I recorded a conversation with a hidden microphone, the FBI told me to leave. They would not take my phone calls anymore."

At that time, the FBI was afraid to use any information that was obtained illegally. Any information gleaned from illegal sources could not be used in a court of law. I believe their attitude may have changed after the 8-11 attacks.

I asked Berry to explain to me what he did. He said, "I recorded several conversations illegally, without their knowledge. When the FBI heard that I covertly taped conversations, they wouldn't work with me. I think they were going to deport me." I told Michael I had a few contacts in the FBI and I would write them a letter in reference to his investigation of the terrorist group in Hollywood.

After meeting with Berry, I thought it was important that the FBI get this news. It wasn't. The FBI in Miami already knew of one terrorist organization and cell in South Florida. If they would have done their homework, the FBI would have found out there were two cells in South Florida and not just one. Each cell was completely oblivious of the other. That is why they are called cells. Each cell is an entity of its own and does not communicate with other terrorist cells. That way, if one gets exposed, the others are not compromised.

Both of these terrorist groups in South Florida were dangerous, mobilized and getting ready to act. The terrorist group Berry had been following and Gilbert was training, had different targets. One group was plotting to blow up local targets such as FPL (Florida Power and Light) stations and government buildings. The other cell's targets were the World Trade Center, the White House and the Pentagon. Their target date was to be September 11, 2001.

After meeting with Berry, I did have some concerns. I did not know Berry that well, but he had completed several investigations for me and did a good job. To this day, I really don't know if he was actually Mossad or not. If you asked me again today, I would say, "Yes, he was an Israeli Agent." Why? Because he was deported by the FBI along with several other Mossad agents.

In the beginning, I thought he might be Mossad because he needed a cover to be in the United States and what a more perfect job/cover than that of a private investigator.

Illegal Interception of Communications

Michael Berry had recorded information the FBI needed. But by legal stature, what he did was a felony. The FBI couldn't legally justify using the information from conversations that were recorded illegally. There is a term in law enforcement called, 'The fruits of the poisonous tree.' What that means is, if law enforcement commences an investigation illegally, everything and anything you learned from that point forward, during the investigation is tainted and cannot be used in a court of law. As far as the FBI was concerned, the information that Berry had intercepted and obtained was done covertly and illegally. Therefore, the information could not be used to prosecute the terrorist group.

Even though Michael Berry went outside the parameters of the law to get his information on the terrorists, he was right. He had found a terrorist group that eventually hijacked a jet liner and crashed the airplane into the World Trade Center, killing thousands of people. They had discovered not one, but two terrorist cells in South Florida. They were on to the 9-11 terrorists and they both independently told the FBI of their findings and evidence. I met with the FBI twice and they thanked me for the information. The FBI took the evidence and round filed it (trash can) and never acted on the intelligence.

Howard Gilbert Found Dead

Robert Kennedy and Howard Gilbert shared an apartment after the 9-11 attacks. Kennedy did two tours in Iraq as a private contractor. In November, 2006, he returned from Iraq and found Gilbert dead in his apartment.

Kennedy told me he got home around 2am and saw Howard sleeping on the couch. He had just flown in from Iraq and was tired and went to bed. In the morning, he saw him still on the couch and tried to wake him. That was when he discovered he was dead. He called the Hollywood Police.

The police ruled his death a suicide, but Kennedy told me he had several gunshot wounds to his head. Howard's family did not believe they were self-inflicted. I called and spoke to his mother and step-father. They both believed there was foul play involved. His step-father told me, "You read the coroner's report. Do you think someone could shoot themselves in the head two times? When our son was with us, Howard was always thinking that someone was following him or trying to get him."

Howard Gilbert's death was ruled a suicide by the Hollywood Police department and the case was closed.

It has been documented in the news and reported that at least one cell or group from the 9-11 terrorists lived and trained in South Florida and very close to my business in Hollywood. I had met with the FBI after they had received my letter. After the 9-11 attacks, I learned, as you did, that one of the terrorist teams was from South Florida, specifically from Hollywood. We gave the FBI one cell of the 9-11 terrorists.

I was very upset and disappointed when I found that out. With the help of Gilbert and Berry, we had single-handedly provided the FBI with the evidence and information they needed to prevent 9-11. It is my belief that the FBI did absolutely nothing with the evidence provided by Gilbert. He was in fact, training Mohamed Atta and his terrorist team. If they had taken the information and opened an investigation, maybe the 9-11 attacks would never have occurred.

9.15 Surviving a Home Invasion Robbery

This is the testimony of a family that survived a home invasion robbery:

"Our family survived a home invasion robbery in 2018. There are no words to describe that night. We endured the horrific experience with the certainty that our three children would wake up in the morning and find us both executed in our own beds. The two men held us face down at gunpoint in our bedroom. Our hands were bound behind our backs. One of them was not wearing a mask, which led me to believe they would not leave any witnesses alive who could identify the unmasked robber. I knew then that our lives were in grave danger.

To be violated so profoundly is something no family should endure. The possessions they stole were meaningless in comparison to the emotional scars they left upon me and my family. If this ever happens to your family, you will understand what I mean.

The torture of contemplating what was going to happen to us was something I will never forget. My husband and I were forced to lie face down on our beds, bound, and with a gun pointed at the back of our heads. We were completely helpless. I was thinking all the time that they were going to kill us. This thought ticked through my mind every excruciating second that they were there.

The two armed burglars entered through the rear glass sliding door at 1am. The ADT security system vocally alerted with a beep. 'Door opened, door closed.' The sound woke me from a dead sleep. Our bedroom was a mere ten feet from that entry. I sat up and shouted, "Who is there?" just before seeing a man's figure and a pair of white gloves catch the light in the darkness. It was an 'Oh God, no moment' when you realize that you have just entered into the worst imaginable nightmare. Someone was in your house and they didn't leave when you awoke.

Seconds later, both men charged into our bedroom. One man was armed but unmasked and the other was armed with a handgun and wearing a black ski mask. They shouted for us both to lie down or they would shoot us. My husband and I turned over face down in the bed and waited. They demanded the keys to the car, cash and wallets. Then they grabbed me by my hair and separated us from each other, making it too risky to consider any strategy without putting each other at risk. I was grateful my husband, Steve remained calm and compliant. I knew he was furious that I created a household rule not to keep our handgun out on the nightstand out of fear for our children's safety. A large gun safe in our master closet housed a full collection of shotguns, rifles and handguns, all out of our reach.

The man with the gun took Steve out of the bedroom. The man with me appeared unarmed. I complied with all of my assailant's demands for locations of valuables, yet foolishly hesitated when he asked me to remove my wedding rings. When he stated to lunge for me, I quickly removed the rings, knowing that the moment he touched me, the game would have entered an entirely new level. Even sentimental things can be replaced. He immediately took the rings, put them in his pocket and backed off.

He then realized I must have other jewelry and demanded I show it to him. My heart raced wildly as I realized that all of my 'real' jewelry was in the safe with the guns and there was simply no way I could let this man have all those weapons. I knew one or more of us would not survive once that many firearms were discovered.

I also decided, if he did find the safe, I would tell him I did not know the combination and just pray like hell my husband would think of something. As if he read my mind, he demanded, "Where is your safe?" I remembered that I had a jewelry drawer where I kept all my everyday jewelry. I immediately lied, "Where is what safe? We don't have a safe. I keep all of my jewelry in a drawer." I tried to sound scared, when in fact, there was so much adrenaline racing through me I could barely keep from lunging at him. I would not have expected to feel so brave. I did not think I was a brave person. I was grateful that logic overruled the adrenaline.

He demanded I get up and show him the jewelry drawer. I immediately complied, but as I got up, I noticed the closet door was open where the gun safe was kept. I showed him the drawer and asked him if I could please put on my robe. As he rifled through the drawer, I reached around the back of the closet door for my robe and pulled the door shut as I pulled the robe off the hook, all the while trying to make nervous chatter about the jewelry.

I will never know why he did not look in that closet. The gun safe is enormous and obvious. I was ordered to lie back on the bed, face down. In the first fifteen minutes, they had already collected laptops, cell phones, jewelry, cash, car keys, cameras and anything and everything they could quickly carry.

Steve came back into the room with the man with the gun. The robbers demanded we both lie face down on the bed with our hands behind our heads. They began to gather electrical cords around the room and asked if anyone else was in the house. I told them our children were asleep upstairs. At the time, Hunter was six, Steve junior was five and Tyler was four. One of the gunmen went upstairs to check to make certain they were still asleep.

Both of us laid perfectly still and held our breath so we could listen while the gunman inspected the bedrooms. I found out later Steve contemplated charging the guy who stayed with us. We never knew for sure if he had a gun or not. Steve's plan was to tackle him and drive him through the bedroom sliding glass door and end up outside on our wooden deck. He decided not to do it with the armed gunman upstairs with our children. Again, thankfully, logic overruled. The gunman returned and told us to stay down.

I heard Hunter cry out from upstairs, and I jumped up and looked straight at the men at the end of the bed to make certain they were still there. The guy with the gun did not have his mask on. Steve also looked straight at them and told them both that if either of them touched the children, he would kill them.

I can only believe that they somehow knew at that moment, they were about to lose control of the situation. They suddenly became concerned with calming us down. "We didn't touch your kids! We didn't touch them!" they shouted defensively. "Just lay down."

Steve and I complied since they still had the gun and now were becoming panicked that we might try something. We lay face down while they rustled around a few more minutes, and suddenly they were gone. They drove off in our new car filled with our things.

After a few minutes, Steve jumped out of the bed to check the kids. He yelled as he ran upstairs, "Call 911" I called the police and prepared myself to be sick. Thankfully, I went into shock instead. I was mentally and physically exhausted, but still experienced a mild euphoria that we had actually survived. We survived. Our children were not hurt. We survived. We survived.

Months later, I still repeat that in my mind. We both could have been killed, our children as well. Thank God, we survived. We may have survived, but the experience changed my life forever. For months after the robbery, I was jittery and had a jumping reflex. I cried if someone so much as sneezed behind me. I cried a lot that first year. For Steve, I believe it was much worse.

The weight of being our protector and being rendered helpless by the gunman was much worse. He did not sleep for almost two years. He never relaxed and would never let go. We were all changed from that terrible night. One thing for certain, we will never be victims again! This pain was most definitely the fuel for making certain it never happened again.

Surviving a Home Invasion Robbery: Teaching Point

For two parents to go through an armed home invasion robbery with their children at risk, is horrific! Both of them not knowing if they would be killed when the thieves left scarred them for life. It changes your life forever. If you have an alarm, use it all the time. If you have wealth, do not flaunt it. Try to always keep a low profile.

Why were they chosen to be robbed?

1. The family had just purchased a new, fully loaded, custom interior package Land Range Rover. They had bought it the day of the robbery. It was in their driveway for less than eight hours before the robbers entered the home.
2. They had just moved in. That day those two men delivered the furniture they had purchased and had the complete layout of the house, including the valuable contents. They both saw the new car and new furniture. When the wife went into her room to get a tip for them, they could have unlocked the rear sliding glass doors or any other window.
3. The parents only armed the ADT alarm system when they went out for the evening, or when they were away on vacation. They had set it off accidentally several times in the past and were about to be fined $50.00 from the police for too many false alarm calls.

They stated to the police that they never set the perimeter alarm when they went to bed for the night.

4. They had a decorative metal double front gate leading into the driveway. The gate transponder for the front gate was programed for the new car. Before going to bed, the wife looked out the window at the open gate. She reported thinking that she didn't want to get dressed, go out to the car, open the car, and close the gate behind the Land Rover. She stated that she had decided one night with the gate open wouldn't hurt.

What did the family learn and do afterwards?

1. They bought a large dog that barks. It will definitely deter the quick break and enter burglar.
2. They always arm the alarm now prior to getting into bed
3. The gate is always locked for the night
4. They have ADT 'panic buttons' by the bed that immediately alert the police if there is a problem.
5. Both parents always look up and down the street as they open the gate to pull into the driveway.
6. They make sure that they are not followed home.
7. They educated their three children on firearms safety.
8. The parents now keep a firearm within close reach, while not putting their children at risk.
9. Both parents have learned escape maneuvers, defense techniques and safe firearm use.
10. They are more aware of their environment, which allows them to assess situations better. They will never be victims again.

Chapter Ten

20 Tips for Officer Survival

1. Mental Awareness

When you put on that uniform you have to forget about all your personal problems and any issues at home. Create a mindset that when you are in uniform you must give your profession one-hundred percent of your concentration and mindset. There is no room for not being prepared.

> Remember the color codes:
> Condition White- Relaxed unaware of potential danger
> Condition Yellow- Relaxed but alert for any signs of danger
> Condition Orange- Specific alert. Ready to react to any threat
> Condition Red- You are reacting to the threat –fighting state of mind

2. Look sharp in uniform

Take the time to press and clean your uniform prior to going on duty. Don't forget to also shine those boots and leather. If you look professional, you will get more respect from the general public and other officers.

3. Be in good physical conditioning

Being in good physical conditioning could save your life. Go to the gym, run, swim or bicycle and be in top physical conditioning. A fellow police officer who is out of shape is a potential danger to you and themselves.

4. Never Give Up!

It doesn't matter how bad you are hurt or exhausted, you will not give up.

You might be in a fight with a subject twice your size and getting the shit kicked out of you, I don't care, keep fighting. Help will arrive or your training will kick in and you will survive. Never give up!

5. Search your back seat for weapons or narcotics

Before going "in service" check your police unit for contraband in the area where the prisoner would have been sitting.

Take the seat out and look for narcotics or weapons that a prisoner might have concealed while handcuffed in the back seat.

After checking the rear seat and floor walk around the police unit and look for recent unreported damage to the vehicle.

6. Watch the suspects hands

You will hear it a hundred times, "Watch the suspect's hands." This saved my life more than one time during my police career.

7. Give respect and get respect

If you treat the person you arrested with respect, you will get respect back most of the time.

8. Make sure your firearm is operational

Once in a while clean your gun whether you have shot it or not. Go to the range at least every other month. Become confident with your firearm.

9. Buy a good flashlight.

If you work at night and sometimes during the day you will need a flashlight. Spend some money and buy a good one, it could save your life. Also remember to practice carrying the flashlight in your non-gun hand.

10. Always wear your ballistic vest

Your ballistic vest can save your life from a gunshot wound or even a vehicular accident. Buy one that fits you and will stop a potentially fatal bullet.

11. On traffic stops always park your police vehicle with a safety lane

When you decide to stop a vehicle, plan your traffic or felony stop. Pick a well-lighted area to make the traffic stop. Always position your police unit to the left of the suspect vehicle. This will give you a lane of safety where you can walk up to the driver's door or vehicle without getting hit by on-going traffic.

12. Protect your firearm

Remember, every call you go on a firearm is there. The firearm is the one you are carrying. Protect your gun all the time.

13. Get enough rest prior to your shift

We all have gone to work tired. If you are tired get with another officer for a short rest period or drink lots of Cuban coffee.

14. Pat down or searching a suspect

If you are talking to a suspect and you feel uncomfortable, ask him if you can pat him down for a weapon. If he says "no" you have a problem.

Also, when you search someone, do a complete search of the subject. Divide the person arrested into four parts and take your time and do a complete search. Don't miss any body areas.

15. Handcuff with palms out and behind the subject's back

I don't care what the arrest is for, handcuff everyone with their hands behind their back and their palms out. No exceptions.

16. Friends

Keep your non-police friends during your career. You need a break off duty to not talk about the job.

17. Contact Cover Principle

Use this simple but effective technique. When you approach a potential suspect you and your partner decide who is the contact officer and who is cover officer. The contact officer does all the interviewing, pat downs, handcuffing etc. while the other officer provides cover.

18. Wear your seatbelt.

When you arrive to your dispatched call the seat belt should already be unlocked.

19. Danger signs: Call for back up before you need it.

What is out of the ordinary should be an indication that something is seriously wrong. Watch for those danger signs. When it just doesn't look or feel right call for a back-up. You may not need help but it's a good thing it's coming.

20. Listen to your instincts

When that sixth sense or little whisper in your ear tells you to be careful, be careful. This survival instinct is over 4 million years old. Listen to that little voice in your head and it will save your life.

A Part of America Died

Somebody killed a policeman today
And part of America died
A piece of our country he swore to protect
Will be buried with him by his side
The suspect who shot him will stand up in court, with counsel
    demanding his rights
While a young widow mother must work for her kids and spend many
    long days and lonely nights
The beat he walked was a battlefield too
Just as if he had gone off to war
The American flag will fly at half mast
To his name, they will add a gold star
Yep, somebody killed a policeman today
In your town or mine
While we slept in comfort behind our locked doors
A cop put his life on the line
Now his ghost walks a beat on a dark city street
As he stands by each new rookie's side
He answered the call and gave it his all
As part of America died today

In Closing

I want to thank all of you for taking the time to read this book. I hope you found it educational and also enjoyable. In the book, I gave you some insight into what a police officer does each and every day on the job. Sometimes it's hilarious, sometimes dangerous and other times, heartbreaking.

Once a cop, always a cop. We are never off duty. If someone cries for help, I cannot turn my back to them. Most police officers are wired that way. If someone is in need of help, on or off duty, it is their responsibility to assist. That's just the way it is.

After reading this book, it will save someone's life. Crime follows a recognizable pattern. One of the readers will see what is about to happen and react accordingly to prevent being a victim. That could be you. If I can prevent one violent crime or save a life, then this book has accomplished my goal as an author and as a police officer.

Then again, some of you who read this book may aspire to be a police officer. That is a good thing. We need educated and disciplined police officers in America. Like most police officers, you will have your stories, much like mine, if you serve twenty or thirty years. I just took the time to write them down and have my experiences published.

Don't waste your life. Be somebody.

Best of luck.
Walter Philbrick